MW00965552

BOOK OF LIES

BOOK OF LIES

**Andrews McMeel
Publishing**

Kansas City

BOOK OF LIES

ISBN-13: 978-0-7407-5560-6
ISBN-10: 0-7407-5560-9

Library of Congress Control Number: 2005929264

05 06 07 08 09 IMA 10 9 8 7 6 5 4 3 2 1

Produced by Essential Works
168a Camden Street, London, NW1 9PT, England

Design by Kate Ward for Essential Works
Layout by Mark Stevens for Essential Works

The publishers have made every reasonable effort to contact all copyright holders. Any errors that may have occurred are inadvertent and anyone who for any reason has not been contacted is invited to write to the publishers so that a full acknowledgment may be made in subsequent editions of this work.

Attention: Schools and Businesses
Andrews McMeel books are available at quantity discounts with bulk purchase for educational, business, or sales promotional use. For information, please write to: Special Sales Department, Andrews McMeel Publishing, 4520 Main Street, Kansas City, Missouri 64111.

INTRODUCTION

This book will make you thin and rich. It will make you irresistible to the opposite sex.

The previous sentence is, of course, a lie. This book is full of lies. Big lies, small lies, preposterous lies, and generous lies. There are also outrageous and hilarious lies. Some of the entries in this book will tell you exactly how a certain lie came to be, who perpetrated it and why. Other entries are outright lies and contain no truth whatsoever. In order to mark those entries out for you, we have assigned them a symbol: ☙.

That you have bought this book shows that you have an interest in truth and lies, as you should in a world that is constantly lying to us, whether to sell something—from clothes to lovers and beyond—or to get us to do something that otherwise we wouldn't (vote Democrat? Republican?). It's getting ever more difficult to tell the truth from that which is not, and we may all need some kind of guide sometimes as to what is a lie and what isn't. Which is where this book comes in.

If it's in here then it's a lie. If it's not in here it might still be a lie, but just not in this book. Sorry. Why not write the publisher to get a second *Book of Lies* into the store soon, so that we can include the lies that are missing? This book marks the beginning of a moral crusade to make this world a straighter place.

People, we have the power to stop the insidious march of mendacity into our lives. If we are forewarned, we are forearmed and can fight the lies that plague us. Read this book, recognize the lies, and you can begin to defeat them as they are pitched against you.

This book will change your life. Buy it now.

I. M. A. Lyre, Editor.

ARE THE LINES STRAIGHT OR WAVY?

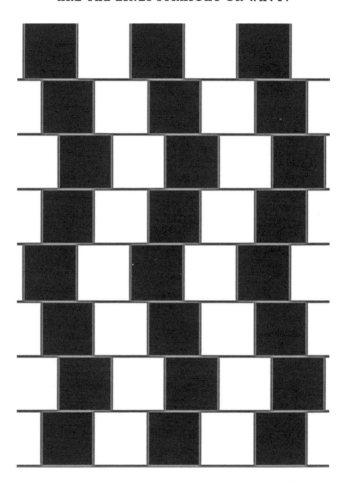

THE TRUTH ABOUT LIARS

Successful liars, or those who have had time to prepare their story, are likely to behave in a very measured and calm manner. They tend to:

Speak slowly (to give themselves time to think)

Maintain eye contact (to check if you believe their story)

Take longer to answer questions (they are not as fluent as truth tellers)

Use fewer gestures (to avoid looking nervous)

Stay calm (to appear trustworthy)

Reply to your questions by repeating them or asking another question. For example, "Did you scrape the side of my car last week?" "Scrape the side of your car? No, of course not." Or "Didn't you go to New York for the weekend with Sally?" "Where on earth did you hear that?"

Use phrases such as: "To tell the truth" or "To be honest . . ."—that is, the opposite of what he or she is saying.

Mismatch facial expressions and words: for example, if someone says "I love you" but has a tense grimace around their mouth and lack of focus in their eyes, you know they're lying. Many facial muscles cannot be consciously controlled, which means that sophisticated observers can recognize when a person is lying. 📖

RADIOACTIVITY LEAK

From 1952, at a government nuclear facility called Hanford Reservation in Richland, Washington, a huge amount of radioactivity was leaking into the air. Local residents were exposed to a quantity of leakage per hour that exceeded levels considered safe for a year. The Atomic Energy Commission were warned by concerned workers who also sent them maps locating the danger areas so that nearby residents could be notified and perhaps evacuated. The AEC opted to ignore the warnings for fear of creating a fuss. ⧗

TOP 10 ROCK LIES

1. Keith Richards has had all his blood changed to combat his drug addiction.
2. Gangsta rap is an expression of the blighted urban environment's rage and frustration against the Establishment.
3. Madonna has made a halfway decent movie.
4. Stevie Wonder's 1973 car crash was a cover story for his going into drug rehab.
5. Liam Gallagher of Britpop band Oasis can hold his drink.
6. Michael Jackson's "Billie Jean" is based on a real person.
7. Punk changed anything.
8. Photographs exist of Mick Jagger, Marianne Faithful, and an erotically positioned Mars bar.
9. Debbie Harry is a natural blonde.
10. Anything remotely interesting ever happens backstage.

THE ARABIC NUMERAL SYSTEM—0, 1, 2, 3, ETC.—ORIGINATED IN ARABIA

Well, that's what the Western world is led to believe. In fact, the numbers that are used today, and which replaced the tedious Roman numeral system, were invented in India in the 7th Century and taken to the Middle East by traders 100 years later. Europeans assumed it to be Arabic because that was where they discovered it.

THE TYPES OF LIES PEOPLE TELL

Lying, according to Nietzsche, is a condition of life. It's almost impossible not to lie, mislead, exaggerate, or be insincere even for a day. In one study, people were found to lie in a fifth of social encounters that lasted 10 minutes or more, and they lied in a third of one-on-one meetings. Attractive, self-confident, extrovert people are more likely to lie, while those with high principles regarding responsibility, close same-sex friendships, or are depressed are least likely to lie.

Lying has evolved as a useful "social lubricant"—you'll get along more smoothly with people if you tell white lies or "false positives" such as "That apple pie was delicious, the nicest I've ever tasted." As well as diplomatic social lies and politeness, which help others feel better about themselves, there are three other kinds of lies. One is "exaggeration": most people want to make themselves sound as interesting and likeable as they can. Being accepted and respected by others makes us feel good, so in everyday encounters we often lie and exaggerate our experiences or importance to impress others. Although this type of lie does not normally hurt others, it can escalate and cause problems for the liar. Exaggerating your golfing proficiency on a job resume, for example, can come back to haunt you when the boss asks you out for a round and discovers you are not really an 8 handicap.

The other two categories of lies are both "malicious" lies, told either to damage someone else, or so that the liar benefits personally from the deception. For example, the characters of Madame de Merteuil and Valmont in Choderlos de Laclos's novel *Les Liaisons Dangereuses* (played by Glenn Close and John Malkovich in the Hollywood film *Dangerous Liaisons*) create a web of lies and distortions in order to seduce and destroy the reputations of two society women. Lying about an affair, on the other hand, is a selfish lie because it protects the liar from potential marital breakdown.

Moral philosophers usually distinguish between social, altruistic "white lies" and destructive, selfish malicious lies, believing the former is mostly acceptable (Plato called them "noble" lies), but the latter—including deliberate fraud and corporate misrepresentation—is not. 📖

THE INDIAN ROPE TRICK

The Indian rope trick was a popular preoccupation in the second half of the 19th century. Accounts of it began by telling of how, according to observers who had visited India, a fakir would throw a piece of rope up into the sky, which, rather than falling down, magically rose up and stayed suspended in the air. Those who purported to see it went on to say that a young boy then climbed the unsupported rope and disappeared into the mist above them. Then the fakir took a sword or dagger, went the story, and followed the boy up the rope. After he too had disappeared from view, there came screams and shouts. Soon after that, body parts, including a head, started to appear from the top of the rope. Then down came the fakir, who put the body parts in one place and threw a cloth over them. Finally, the fakir removed the cloth and—hey presto—the boy reappeared, back together again.

For more than a century people have tried to work out how this trick was performed. Suggestions have varied wildly. Some believed the trick involved mass hypnosis or levitation. The rope was thrown over a length of invisible wire tied to trees or hills or buildings, others ventured. The body parts were those of a shaved monkey and they were hidden under the fakir's cloak, it was suggested. Or the boy was one of twins and one was actually killed. Something about this trick captured the public imagination after it first appeared in the *Chicago Tribune* on 8 August 1890, and newspapers were soon full of the separate, individual accounts of people—around 50 of them—who said they had seen the trick performed in India. Interest kept gathering pace.

The British Magic Circle, however, were not convinced the trick even existed, and offered 500 guineas to anyone who could perform it. The upshot was a number of attempts. Footage was made that claimed to be of the trick being performed but none of it was accepted as genuine. A film was made by psychic investigator of the 1920s and 1930s Harry Price, which showed Karachi, a British performer, performing the first part of the trick in a field near Hatfield in Hertfordshire, but the Magic Circle would not part with the money because the boy—Karachi's son—did not vanish. More obvious hoaxes involved rope that clearly had a pole behind it or reversed film, which made the falling rope look like it was rising.

So what of the eyewitness accounts? In *The Rise of the Indian Rope Trick*, author Peter Lamont established that there were five types of account: 1) the boy climbs up the rope, 2) the boy vanishes at the top and then reappears, 3) the boy vanishes and doesn't come back, 4) the boy vanishes and reappears somewhere else, 5) the boy disappears and reappears somewhere that was in full view all the time. No account involved decapitation or severed limbs, but most interesting of all, the more years that had lapsed between seeing the trick and giving an account of it, the more impressive was the story. Although the witnesses had seen tricks that resembled the Indian rope trick, the automatic human response seemed to be exaggerated over time.

Another rarer impulse has also played a part whereby if a story is repeated as true enough times, people will believe it despite evidence to the contrary and even denials from its alleged creator. During his research into the trick, in a corner of a *Chicago Tribune* dated 4 months after the one introducing it, Lamont found an editorial note that seemed to solve the matter for good. It was a confession from the newspaper that the Indian rope trick was a hoax. It expressed surprise at the number of people who had believed it, pointing out that the byline was pretty blatant: Fred S. Ellmore. But by then the genie was out of the bottle. ⧖

LOVE CHEAT LIES #1

If you hear more than three of these in one week, get suspicious. You may be living with an infidel.

"I'm almost home but first I've got to stop off somewhere . . ."—If he or she is vague about *where* they are stopping off, this is a blatant lie. It isn't as if they are going to stop off at Tiffany's and get you a large diamond ring or anything. Come off it. They're either cheating on you or they're down at the bar, knocking back brewskis. The point is that they are not coming home to you. It almost doesn't matter if they are sleeping with someone else or drinking themselves into a stupor: they'd rather do that than be home with your happy little face.

❋ ❋ ❋

"I have to work late."—This only works if there is some semblance of truth in their voice, a sound of distress or disturbance. Working late for many nights in a row, without obvious signs of a deadline or group project, bodes badly in the romance department. Work is a place to leave, not stay at. Work is the ideal excuse because 1) the switchboard could be down, 2) there is a good chance you will think they are working alone and so there would be nothing untoward going on, and 3) you don't want to upset or bother them if they really are in a deadline crisis. On the other hand, if they are not in the building and seeing someone else, unanswered emails and cell phone calls are certainly a tip-off unless . . .

❋ ❋ ❋

"My computer crashed."—This is no longer a good reason not to get an email. There are wireless connections all over and, with the prevalence of

laptops, handhelds, etc., communication has never been easier. If the computer crashed, the only reason you wouldn't be able to get through to them would be 1) if they used a program-based email account that was accessible from only one machine, and 2) they were too annoyed trying to fix the thing to answer any phones that were around, unless 3) they were in a signal-proof area and their cell didn't work. Let's face it: the probability of those things happening in sequence is lower than that of your partner having an affair. As technology enables us to get in touch faster, easier, and better, cheaters will have fewer and fewer tech-based excuses.

※ ※ ※

"How did I know about the shoe sale? Oh, er, I can't remember. . . . It must have been Jack at the office."—An out and out lie. Any time your beloved starts talking about odd topics that seem abnormal—your boyfriend knows about an obscure sale or your girlfriend knows about a car part—it could be that their lover-information-center isn't working properly. New styles of clothes, fragrance, restaurant, and, of course, sex patterns are also a dead giveaway. Such as . . .

※ ※ ※

"I find you irresistible these days."—You are irresistible because he or she is getting more sex somewhere else, which is ramping up their entire libido. This means that while you are getting more of the good stuff, you are getting his/her lover's sexual run-off. You're not getting more sex because you're good at it or are so sexy your partner can't handle being around you. They're having more sex with you because they are thinking and fantasizing about someone else. More sex, different sex, *better* sex? Look out. ❀

CLOWNFISH ARE FUNNY

Brightly colored? Yes. Amusing? Not even if you're very bored. 🖥🖊

A STICKY MOMENT

After shooting the cover for The Ohio Players' album *Honey*, it took five hours to detach the model from the photographer's studio floor, as after the hot lights were switched off the honey she was covered in set firm. 🖥🖊

ALCOHOLIC LIES OR TRUTH

Lie: Black coffee will sober you up.
Truth: All it does is give you a caffeine jolt, which will turn a sleepy drunk into a wide-awake drunk—which do you think is more dangerous?

Lie: Anybody can drink themselves sober.
Truth: The more alcohol you introduce to your system the more drunk you will become, and the occasional moments of pie-eyed "clarity," which are bound to occur during a heavy session, should never be confused with sobriety.

Lie: Diabetics mustn't drink. At all.
Truth: They can drink moderately, as a large amount of alcohol in one session will impair the liver's response to blood sugar levels, and the body will be unable to react swiftly if the levels are dangerously high or low. Also, diabetics need to be aware of the amount of sugar occurring in alcohol.

Lie: Women can out-drink men.
Truth: There must be a few out there who can, but there is an enzyme that breaks down alcohol before it can saturate the bloodstream and men have 4 times more of this than women.

Lie: You won't get a hangover drinking vodka.
Truth: Yes you will, because the main cause of a hangover is dehydration, and that will be due to the amount of alcohol you consume whatever the type. Vodka's only advantage is that it contains fewer of the mildly-toxic contributing congeners than its darker contemporaries.

Lie: A nightcap will help your sleep.
Truth: It may immediately relax you, but in 2 or 3 hours the sugar in the drink will have been metabolized and cause a rush that will either wake you up or greatly disrupt your sleep pattern. 💾

TOP 10 LIES OUR CHILDREN TELL US

It wasn't me
I didn't do it
It was already broken
I didn't eat it
I made it all by myself
Nowhere
No one
He/She made me do it
I'll pay for it
I'll do it in a minute ✿

HOLLYWOOD MYTHS EXPLODED

Richard Pryor burned himself while freebasing cocaine.
The 1980 fire that burned 50 percent of the comedian's body happened after he poured high-proof rum over himself and set it alight, in a stoned suicide attempt (he'd been freebasing for several days).

Donald Sutherland and Julie Christie actually "did it" in *Don't Look Now*.
At the time (1973) this rumor was a publicist's dream, but it was never true.

Marilyn Monroe never used to wash, bathe, or take a shower.
The persistent rumor was that the closest she came to personal hygiene was bleaching her pubic hair to match her coif up top, but this was never true.

Phil Collins robbed banks.
When the former Genesis drummer and solo singing star was getting into character to play the Great Train Robber Buster Edwards in the 1988 movie *Buster*, he held up post offices and banks.

Gene Hackman could have directed *The Silence Of The Lambs*, but he thought it was too big a project for his directorial debut.
Actually, he thought that it was much too violent. 🖫

F FOR FAKE

The exotically named Elmyr de Hory fooled the art world for 30 years. Born, equally exotically, Elmyr Dory-Boutin in Hungary in 1905, his parents were Jewish and solidly middle class enough (father an ambassador, mother from a banking family) to have their son raised chiefly by governesses. Yet Elmyr was not destined to be part of the establishment and was to lead a very colorful and eventful life.

After beginning his art studies in Munich, in 1926 he moved to Paris where he studied under Fernand Léger. He returned to Hungary, but during WWII he claimed to have been in a concentration camp and then a Berlin hospital from which he escaped, returning to Hungary where his parents had been killed by the Nazis and all his family's property and possessions seized. Elmyr made his way to France where he began to make a living as a painter.

In 1946, he sold a reproduction of a Picasso to a British acquaintance who believed it to be an original. Realizing he had a talent for artistic mimicry, he painted some more Picassos and sold them to galleries for modest sums. Later that same year he went into partnership with Jacques Chamberlin who acted as a dealer for his forgeries. They traveled extensively across Europe, but finding that Chamberlin had been cheating him out of his full share of the profits, in 1947 Elmyr decided to ditch him and go it alone. He began to branch out and imitate other artists with many "new found" works by Picasso, Toulouse-Lautrec, Modigliani, Dufy, and Matisse, among others.

By the 1950s he was living in Miami, and was known as a successful art dealer. but the art world was beginning to get suspicious. First a "Matisse" sold to the Fogg Art Museum was investigated, and then suspicions were aroused again in 1955 when Chicago art dealer Joseph W. Faulkner was astute enough to spot the fakes. But Elmyr was proving to be Teflon coated. Nothing stuck. He continued to forge his way across the world avoiding both Interpol and the FBI, although in 1968 he had a 2-month sojourn in a Spanish jail in Ibiza, charged with homosexuality and consorting with criminals. The following year, Clifford Irving told Elmyr's life story in *Fake*. Irving was obviously bitten by the forgery bug as he went on to indulge in a little scam of his own when he faked the autobiography of Howard Hughes a few years later.

By the 1970s Elmyr had become quite famous. He went on TV and appeared in Orson Welles's 1974 film *F for Fake* which told the story of his life. It was around this time that Elmyr decided to try painting again in his own style and he managed to support himself in a modest way. However, he discovered that the French wanted to extradite him on charges of fraud and knew that if convicted he would probably spend the rest of his life in prison. He was found dead in his home in Ibiza in December 1976, having apparently taken an overdose of sleeping tablets. Friends said that he had been depressed, but some claimed that he had even faked his own suicide, although this seems unlikely. During his lifetime Elmyr claimed to have sold over 1,000 modern art fakes all over the world. ✎

SURVIVAL TIPS THAT MAY (OR MAY NOT) WORK

In a confrontation with a tiger, it will be more scared of you than you are of it.

If you are attacked by a great white shark, throw powdered turmeric in its eyes and it will turn tail and swim away.

If confronted with a hungry lion, show no fear and it will leave you alone. 🗦🖢

NEW AGE LIES #1

There are among us people who have discovered a form of spirituality and peace that does not come from the old, organized religions, but from something called New Age teachers. Horribly, somehow New Age teachings have become common practice among otherwise normal-seeming people. Sadly, these people are forever attempting to pass on their "wisdom" to the unenlightened among us. So, whenever you are faced with a New Age disciple trying to "convert" you to their way of thinking, answer their lies thus:

※ ※ ※

"Follow your joy and money will come."—Or the bailiffs will come, one or the other. Of course, it is true that if you love something, you will be more likely to succeed in it and possibly get paid to do it. But if you just like to pick the lint out of your toes, if that's where your joy is, then you and the universe aren't going to get along very well.

※ ※ ※

"What you think is what you become."—If you think you are a success, all you have to do is convince everyone else that you are too. Thinking positively will make you more pleasant to be around, but being a little too positive can work against you. People will think you are hiding something—and so you are.

※ ※ ※

"I am moving toward prosperity and happiness."—How can you be sure you are moving in this direction? And even if you are, will you reach it before you shuffle off? That is the trouble with affirmations: you can program your mind to shoot right past your goals or to move them far out of your reach with the wrong verb tense. Be careful of the subjunctive: the unconscious mind hates that.

※ ※ ※

"The universe is unfolding as it should."—While not strictly speaking a lie, it is a nonsense statement. As if you had any say over it. There is no other alternative. Your life will have ups and downs, good things and bad things. Your decisions don't really matter much in this crazy world. The universe is unfolding. It is unfolding right on your freshly washed laundry and it doesn't care. ✿

THE PROTOCOLS OF THE ELDERS OF ZION

This forged document inspired and reinforced European anti-Semitism in the early years of the 20th century. It was supposed to be an account of secret meetings held in 1897 at a Zionist Congress in Basel, Switzerland. In it, a Jewish cabal planned to achieve world power primarily through the domination of international finance. Christian society would be undermined and a single world state established, governed jointly by Jews and Freemasons. The Protocols were first published in a Russian newspaper in 1903 that claimed to have uncovered "A Program for World Conquest by the Jew." A fuller version was printed 2 years later in a religious tract by the Russian writer, Sergei Nilus. In fact, the Protocols had been compiled by the Tsarist secret police, drawing extensively, it later emerged, on mid-19th century French political satire and the 1868 novel *Biarritz* by Hermann Goedsche. They were disseminated widely: a copy was found in the possession of Tsar Nicholas II in 1918, and in the United States, extracts from the Protocols were published in Henry Ford's anti-Semitic newspaper *The Dearborn Independent*. Although the Protocols were exposed as fraudulent in the 1920s, their influence proved durable. Copies are still in circulation in the Middle East and amongst neo-fascist groups. ᴖ

ENTERTAINMENT LIES

If you want to record in Nashville and you don't wear a cowboy hat, you can be shot at. No questions asked.

Jennifer Lopez is so pleased with the fame and fortune her butt has brought her that she has left it $10 million in her will.

Jon Bon Jovi is frightened of lobsters, which is why it's rare to see crustacea of any sort in his videos. 🖫◖

DON'T EAT FOR AN HOUR BEFORE SWIMMING

It's written in stone for parents, it's an early lesson in patience for children, and it's a load of rubbish. Everybody knows that you are not supposed to swim for an hour after eating or you get life-threatening cramps and risk drowning, right? Actually, it ain't so.

Where this urban myth originated is not clear, but there is no medical evidence to back it up. Perhaps it should be consigned to the file marked "conspiracy theory." Presumably it all started on a family holiday when a quick-witted mother or father who wanted to relax on the beach after lunch, and possibly have a little snooze, needed an excuse to keep the kids close rather than having to keep an eye on them swimming. In a single stroke of genius they, and countless parents since, were saved, if only for an hour, from the responsibility, the inane waving, the drips, and the comedy seaweed down the back routine. ⧗

3 TIMES A LADY

Ann Marrow clearly thought that 18th-century England was a man's world and as such she would be better off living in it as a man. However, she took her gender bending a step too far when she decided to not only dress as a man, but also to get married to a woman not once but 3 times in all. Adept at defrauding her hapless "wives" of their money and goods, she was evidently less convincing in her masculine guise and was found out. Sentenced to 3 months imprisonment in 1777, she was obliged to take a turn in the pillory at Charing Cross where she lost the sight in both eyes thanks to the skillful aim of the baying crowd. It was reported that it was the women who pelted her the most assiduously. ✎

OLD LADY/YOUNG LADY OPTICAL ILLUSION

Glamorous young woman dressed in furs or wrinkled old hag?

LIES WE TELL OURSELVES #1

As much as we may tell untruths to the government, our parents, partners, or children, we may also tell ourselves lies. Because we have to, and because it makes us feel better about ourselves.

"I'll do it tomorrow."—Procrastination is a lie because, unless there is arterial spray involved or the IRS, things don't get done tomorrow or maybe ever. The grass isn't mown, the car isn't fixed, the button isn't sewn on, the dog isn't washed. What does get done is the fun stuff such as watching your favorite TV show, playing a new game, or lounging on the sofa doing absolutely nothing. By merely telling ourselves that we will get around to doing some important thing, it is as if we have put the item on a mental "to do" list. Once it is on our list, we think it will get done. Actually, the task we are avoiding often stays on the list, sliding down in priority until we have missed the deadline, allowed someone else to do it, or given up on the whole procedure. The person who thinks tomorrow is the day to do things but never gets around to them is the person who lives in their own filth. And nobody likes them.

"Nobody talks to me like that!"—Well, actually, everybody talks to you like that! You're only saying they don't to quell your fears. Allowing yourself to be dissed or insulted in a social situation is, sadly, part of social situations and their inherent hierarchy. One of the perversities of human culture is the fact that he who puts others down verbally is often seen as the master of the group. By kicking against the group structure—"nobody talks to me like that!"—you are showing others that you have no idea what your role is within the group. The wise person takes the hit and keeps going rather than reacting to it. Also, reacting or striking out when someone bullies you, say, will often result in a black eye. So, actually, the social survivor allows almost everyone to talk to them any way they darned well please.

"Nobody is the winner in this situation."—It is the myth of the modern "happy office" that we are all working toward universal happiness. Our deals and agreements must strive to be "win-win," i.e., good for you and good for me. The worst case scenario of this "win-win" culture is the "no-win" category, where no one gets what they want, everyone is unhappy and the deal leaves a bad taste in the mouths of all involved. Often, we take comfort in telling ourselves that some situation or other couldn't have had a different outcome and that, in fact, no one made any gains there. This is rarely the case. We merely tell ourselves that nobody won when, in essence, it was only *we* who didn't profit from the situation, financially or otherwise. This is yet another one of the little lies we tell ourselves about

our capacity as dealmakers and deal breakers. Truly, someone wins something. Just as truthfully, it is not, in this case, you. The comfort-taking lie exists merely as an analgesic, a sort of verbal and mental aspirin for the headache of disappointment.

"I think I handled that well."—Alarm bells should ring when you say such self-congratulatory statements. This is a sign that your inner censor, that little mind's eye that watches the proceedings of your life with a more detached view, is metaphorically tugging at your sleeve. You may have handled a certain situation, yes, but maybe not as well as you would have liked. You have shown a hand that, perhaps subconsciously, you feel you've goofed.

"I think I got away with it."—Don't breathe a sigh of relief just yet. This is the sort of thing said before the police arrive on the doorstep. Stealing something, having unprotected sex, telling a damaging lie to someone . . . all of these actions may be ones that you hope you will get away with—the kind you hope other people won't notice. But be warned, you may be reassuring yourself with a lie. And if you have to lie to yourself about the potential consequences of your actions, perhaps your actions need to be re-examined. Or maybe you need to be sneakier in the future. ❁

NOT WHO THEY SAY THEY ARE #1

For some reason many famous musicians have chosen to drop the name that their parents gave them, and replace it with something that they feel is far more "fitting." With some artists the decision was undoubtedly a good one—see Lou Reed—while for others you have to ask, why bother?

IS NOW	WAS ONCE
Adam Ant	Stuart Goddard
Pat Benatar	Pat Andrejewski
Gary "U.S." Bonds	Gary Anderson
Bono	Paul Hewson
David Bowie	David Jones
50 Cent	A. Dime
Ray Charles	Ray Robinson
Eric Clapton	Eric Clapp
Alice Cooper	Vince Furnier
Ice Cube	O'Shea Jackson
Bobby Darin	Walden Cassotto
John Denver	Henry Deutschendorf Jr.
Bo Diddley	Elias Bates
Bob Dylan	Robert Zimmerman
The Edge	David Evans
Marvin Gaye	Marvin Gay
Macey Gray	Natalie McIntyre
Buddy Holly	Charlie Holley
Janis Ian	Janis Fink
Billy Idol	William Broad
Elton John	Reg Dwight
Tom Jones	Tom Woodward
Chaka Khan	Yvette Stevens
Queen Latifah	Dana Owens
LL Cool J	James Todd Smith
Barry Manilow	Barry Pincus
Manfred Mann	Michael Lubowitz
George Michael	Georgios Panayiotou
Van Morrison	George Ivan
Nico	Crista Pavolsky

IS NOW	WAS ONCE
Iggy Pop	James Osterberg
P. J. Proby	James Marcus Smith
Dee Dee Ramone	Douglas Colvin
Joey Ramone	Jeff Hyman
Johnny Ramone	Johnny Cummings
Tommy Ramone	Tom Erdelyi
Lou Reed	Lou Firbank
Busta Rhymes	Trevor Smith Jr.
Axl Rose	William Bailey
Slash	Saul Hudson
Dusty Springfield	Mary O'Brien
Donna Summer	La Donna Gaines
David Sylvian	David Batt
Sid Vicious	John Ritchie
Bunny Wailer	Neville Livingston
Muddy Waters	McKinley Morganfield

THE VENUS FLYTRAP

Many plant and animal species look or smell enticing in order to deceive the unwary. The Venus flytrap attracts insects to the sweet-smelling nectar on the leaves that form the trap. When an insect touches the hair triggers on the leaves, they snap shut around it, and it is then broken down and digested by the plant. Angler fish (also known as monkfish) sit on the bottom of the seabed and attract prey by waving long anterior rays above their huge, hidden mouths—when a fish comes by to investigate, the angler fish lunges out and grabs it. 🌱

TOP 10 HEALTH LIES

1. An apple a day keeps the doctor away.
2. Always put a dead badger on a head wound.
3. You can cure a rheumatic joint if you get bees to sting it.
4. Fat people are happy people.
5. No pain, no gain.
6. Men are more susceptible than women to diabetes.
7. Red wine is good for you.
8. The French don't die of heart attacks.
9. Doctors are taught to write like that, because if you knew what they were actually prescribing you'd never go and see one again.
10. Wearing suntan lotion will prevent skin cancer. 🖫🌢

WHAT MAKES A LEADER GREAT

For the last 5 years of his life Ronald Reagan ate nothing but cheese.

Nelson Mandela has 11 toes.

Tony Blair's ears go red when he tells an untruth.

George W. Bush is a psychopathic liar and has passed several staged lie detector tests.

Paul Wolfowitz suffers from Dyscalculia. Hitler was a vegetarian and intended for the Third Reich to become vegan. 🖫🌢

CHICKEN FEED

Mass-produced chicken pieces may only contain just over 50 percent chicken, with the rest of the weight made up from water and bits of other animals such as pigs and cows. Chicken pieces have, for a long time, been injected with water prior to sale to bulk them up and (so manufacturers claim) to stop them drying out during cooking. More recently though, thanks to the development of something called hydrolyzed protein, the proportion of water has gone up dramatically. These are proteins rendered by treating unusable animal carcass waste—bone, hooves, ligaments, skin, feathers—to very high temperatures, then, when added to the chicken flesh, they swell it up and enable it to hold proportionately far more water—up to 50 percent.

Astonishingly, one of the secret ingredients routinely found in factory-farmed chicken is arsenic. It is a component of the increasingly powerful antibiotics that lace modern chicken feed, and is vital to limit the bacterial infections that can spread like wildfire among the crowded conditions in which factory-raised hens live.

However, the arsenic gets passed on to humans—around 4 micrograms per portion isn't unusual—where it has been linked with cancer and nervous system complaints.

During the last 50 years—since factory farming techniques began to evolve—the average period needed for an eating chicken (as opposed to an egg-layer) to grow to full size has been reduced by one third, from 63 days to 42 days. And the amount of food required has been halved from 7 lbs to 3.5 lbs.

Chicken nuggets are largely made of chicken skin.

Egg producers don't have to tell you if their eggs are from battery hens, and such labeling as "Farmyard" or "Natural Fresh" or "Country Fresh" are meaningless. However, they can't call them "Free Range" if they're not. 💾

IF EVERYBODY TRIED TO USE THE INTERNET AT THE SAME TIME . . .

The energy created would knock the Earth off its axis. This is already starting to happen, which is why we don't get "proper" seasons any more. 💾♦

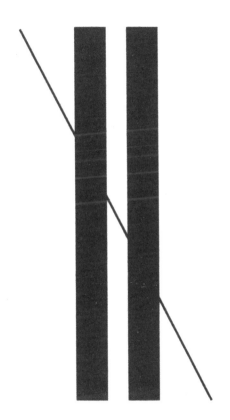

The diagonal line in this diagram is straight. Truth or lie?

HOW TO SPOT A LIAR TALKING

We all have occasion to meet with or talk to a liar. Hopefully that liar is not a family member, because it's harder for us to believe that anyone who shares our genes could possibly lie convincingly and often, thus making it much more difficult to tell when we're being lied to. Countless magazine articles have been published that make claims about spotting a liar because their body language will give them away. Well-practiced liars know how to control those normally reflexive physical tics that signal a lie. However, it is true that it's often not what they say, but the way they say it. Researchers have found some linguistic habits that liars tend to use or avoid:

They use fewer first-person singular pronouns, such as "I," "me," or "my." This is because at an unconscious level they want to dissociate themselves and not "own" the lie.

They use fewer "exclusive" words, which define difference and distinction (such as "but," "although," and "except"), and more inclusive terms (like "every," "often," and "all"). Telling lies is a complicated cognitive process, and psychologists suggest that having to mentally determine what they were not meant to be doing as well as what they were meant to be doing during the lie is too complex. So liars use inclusive, vague concepts such as "I was there all morning as I often am" instead of "I left at 11.15 A.M. Saturday." This also makes their story harder to pin down.

They use more words with negative emotions, such as "hate" and "angry." It's thought that deceiving others heightens emotions such as guilt and anxiety, so people express more negative emotions when they are not telling the truth.

They use more words indicating motion, such as "move," "run," "walking," and "going." Psychologists are not sure why but speculate that this might be to move the story along and create a momentum that stops listeners from enquiring more deeply.

They don't tend to abbreviate words—they will say "I did not go to Richard's house" rather than "I didn't go . . ." In fact, one study showed that if someone is contracting their verbs, they are 60 percent more likely to be telling the truth.

They use vague terms including fewer factual statements and past-tense verbs—perhaps to avoid being caught out in specific contradictions that can be disproved. 📖

LIES WOMEN TELL MEN #1

In the seemingly never-ending battle of the sexes, which wages all around us and constantly, there are some things that never change. That members of the opposite sex will tell each other lies is one of the constants of human relationships. Listed here are some of those lies that men can expect to hear at some point if they are romantically involved or otherwise find themselves in a relationship with a woman. Be prepared.

✳   ✳   ✳

"I am on the pill."—The lie that really means, "I want your baby." Any woman who tells you that she is on the pill probably isn't. Otherwise, why would she say that she is? Unless you know her very well, she will want you *not* to know she is on the pill for obvious health reasons. Be aware and be suspicious for this particular bit of unwarranted honesty. There's something behind it and that something is invariably paternity. Unless you're keen on knitting booties and paying for schooling, keep things in your wallet for the weekend when you hear a lie like this.

✳   ✳   ✳

"No, I wasn't waiting for you to call."—The lie that means, "What took you so darned long?" Women will always be waiting for your call, even if she says she isn't. They can't help themselves. The minute they hear the words "call" and "you" together, they automatically set up a nest near the phone—ice cream, tissues, vodka, cigarettes, two cats—and await you to let them down by not calling. If you do call, they will feel relief and disgust. They will believe in the goodness of human nature as surely as they will believe you are a putz for actually calling when you say you will.

✳   ✳   ✳

"I am not seeing anyone else."—The lie that means, "I am seeing the football team really but who's to know?" Any woman who tells this lie knows she is popular and knows, frankly, that she probably had you at the phrase, "You're standing on my foot." She has more male attention—and possibly female hatred—than she can handle. Nevertheless, she wants your adoration. The trouble is she wants *everyone's* adoration. Unless this is an answer to a direct question, do not take her at face value. Many other people have and will. ✽

MARY TOFT'S OFFSPRING

In September 1726, British physician John Howard was called to attend Mary Toft in Godalming as she was giving birth. On arrival he was somewhat surprised to find Mary giving birth, but to rabbits. Unfortunately the rabbits were not only dead but were in pieces. Mary explained that she had had a craving for rabbit meat during her recent pregnancy and had subsequently dreamt that rabbits were gamboling about in her lap.

Howard sought the opinions of some eminent colleagues and Mary was required to bring bunnies into the world in their presence. She obliged, and although the offspring were dead and in pieces as before, the assembled doctors were amazed.

News spread and Mary became famous. She was brought to London, but once she was placed under constant supervision, the curve of the bunny birthrate graph took a steep downward turn. Mary realized she was about to be found out when the London physician, Sir Richard Manningham, offered to carry out a surgical internal examination on her. Since this was not a pleasant prospect in 18th-century London, Mary owned up—she had placed parts of dead rabbits inside her body.

Mary was sent to jail for fraud, though she was soon released and later gave birth, this time to one of her own species. She was immortalized in one of William Hogarth's engravings entitled, *Credulity, Superstition, and Fanaticism*. John Howard, who had first brought Mary to the world's attention, fared less well and his career ended in ruin. ✒

HOW TO SPOT A MEDIEVAL LIAR

Anyone suspected in medieval times of lying had to submit to a "trial by ordeal" of fire or water, presided over by a member of the clergy. The accused would have to carry a red-hot iron bar in their hand for nine paces, plunge his hand into a pot of boiling water to retrieve a stone, or walk over nine ploughshares, which had also been heated until they were red hot. The idea was that God would help the innocent through the ordeal. The wound was bound and if it had healed after three days the accused was pronounced innocent, but if, as was more often the case, the flesh was still burned, they were pronounced guilty and punished.

If water was chosen for the test, the accused was bound and thrown into a river or pond. If they sank they were innocent, but if they floated they were guilty. Again, the hapless suspect stood a strong chance of dying either way—if they were not fished out quickly enough once they had sunk, or if found guilty the punishment was death. Doubtless unwilling to submit themselves to such a painful ordeal, members of the clergy suspected of lying simply had to eat a piece of cheese, bread, or cake while reciting a prayer exhorting God to make them choke if they were guilty.

This medieval form of lie detection was forbidden in 1215 by an edict issued by the Fourth Lateran Council, a series of meetings held between the pope and other dignitaries of the Catholic Church. Henry III duly abolished trial by ordeal in England in 1219, replacing it with trial by jury. ✎

THE WEAPONS

OF MASS DESTRUCTION.

EUGENICS DEEP IN THE AMAZON

It is a story of the very most sinister Frankenstein kind. A story which confirms the worst fears of the masses about genetics. In the mid-1960s, U.S. geneticist James Neel was working in the homeland of the Yanomami Indians in Venezuela and Brazil. His work was funded by the U.S. Atomic Energy Commission—an organization whose area of interest was the consequences for communities of nuclear war.

The Yanomami had already suffered pollution and disease as a result of the influx of gold miners and timber producers, but according to journalist Patrick Tierney, James Neel's objective was now to harm them deliberately. In an attempt to test the effects of natural selection on "primitive societies," and without the Yanomami knowing,

he vaccinated them with a measles vaccine.

This caused an epidemic that killed hundreds, probably thousands of Yanomami. Researchers were told only to record the results and not to help the sick. Neel had a theory that in such isolated communities an epidemic would eventually allow genetically superior, dominant males to reproduce, thus improving the stock. He was only concerned with finding out by experiment whether he was right.

There are now around 21,000 Yanomami in the Amazon rainforest, but their numbers are thought to be decreasing by about 13 percent per year as a result of environmental changes brought about by outsiders plundering their resources. ⏳

MARLBORO CIGARETTES ARE FUNDING
THE KU KLUX KLAN

If you take one of the crushproof packs from the regular cartons apart, the red and white design reconfigures to form the initials KKK. ☙

THE MAN WHO NEVER WAS

On 30 April 1943, the body of a Major Martin of the Royal Marines, killed in an air crash, was washed up on the shore of Spain. Chained to his body was a briefcase containing secret documents relating to Allied Mediterranean operations. Although Franco's Spain was officially neutral, the information on the body was passed to the Germans, who celebrated a major intelligence coup. However, the coup actually belonged to the British. Major Martin never existed, and the body used by the British was probably that of John Melville, a Scottish sailor who had drowned on HMS *Dasher* in the Firth of Clyde on 27 March. His remains were taken to Spain and slipped into the sea, complete with the bogus identification and documents indicating that the Allies were planning an invasion of Sardinia and southern Greece. The letters set out a strategy by which these attacks would be masked by preparations for an apparent assault on Sicily. This was a masterful double bluff: Sicily was the real Allied target. ✍

THERE IS A SECRET TUNNEL

Under the Atlantic connecting the U.K. and Greenland. It was built just after World War II in case an invasion threatened again and Britain needed to be evacuated. 📖💣

NAZI MONOPOLY MONEY

In 1942 SS Major Bernhard Kruger came up with a plan to try and destabilize enemy economies by flooding them with counterfeit banknotes.

The Nazis scoured the concentration camps to find the most highly skilled artists and printers and put them to work. "Operation Bernhard" was launched. By the end of the war, the equivalent of an estimated $7 billion in today's terms of Nazi Monopoly money had been forged at a camp at Sachsenhausen near Berlin. Despite it being mostly in British pounds sterling the Germans managed to get relatively little of it into circulation in Britain. Instead the majority was used to finance espionage and pay collaborators in countries where pounds sterling could easily be converted into native currency. It also enabled the Nazi bigwigs to indulge the artistic sides of their natures by adding to their art collections, of course. ✍

LEARNED LYING #1: DECODING LEGAL LIES

As anyone who has ever dealt with a lawyer can tell you, just because it's in Latin doesn't mean that it's the truth. Smart words and phrases to be used in the pursuit of the untruth.

ARGUMENTUM AD NUMERAM:
Meaning: The more people who believe something the larger the possibility of it being true; e.g., "Well, everyone believes I didn't take your wallet." Problem with use: Seems like an excuse already.

ACCENTUS:
Meaning: Emphasizing a word or phrase, therefore making it ambiguous or misleading; e.g., "I did not *take* the money from your wallet." Problem with use: emphasis usually causes suspicion. "If you didn't *take* it, what *did* you do?"

ARGUMENTUM AD ANTIQUITAM:
Meaning: An old rule is a good rule; e.g., "Money is the root of all evil so you should give me the root of your evil." Problem with use: Requires other person to respect the old rules.

ARGUMENTUM AD BACULUM:
Meaning: The old "offer you can't refuse"; e.g., "I'll whack you if you don't give me your wallet." Major problem with use: Violence.

ARGUMENTUM AD CRUMENAM:
Meaning: The golden rule—whoever has the gold makes the rules; e.g., "I have more money than you so I am smarter and would look after yours better than you would." Problem with use: Makes people without money defensive.

ARGUMENTUM AD HOMINEM:
Meaning: Discrediting the person rather than what they're saying/doing; e.g., "Why, you're so idiotic that any money you spend is wasted!" Problem with use: Will stick in their mind forever.

ARGUMENTUM AD IGNORANTIAM:
Meaning: If it cannot be proven to be false, it must be true; e.g., "You can't prove I took your money so I didn't." Problem with use: Can make people seek proof.

ARGUMENTUM AD LAZARUM:
Meaning: If you're poor, you have a better chance of speaking the truth; e.g., "Why would I take money from your wallet? I am poor but I'm proud."

Problem with use: Anachronistic ideal that no longer holds in Western cultures.

ARGUMENTUM AD MISERICORDIAM:

Meaning: Using pity to get what you want; e.g. "I am so poor that you should give me money from your wallet, for God's sake." Problem with use: Don't wear Armani during use.

ARGUMENTUM AD NAUSEUM:

Meaning: A statement is more likely to be true if you hear it a lot; e.g., "I am poor. You are not. I should have your wallet now. I am poor. You are not. I should have your wallet now . . ." Problem with use: The stronger people will steel themselves against repetition. On the good side, repetition can often wear people down.

ARGUMENTUM AD NOVITAM:

Meaning: If it is new, then it must be true; e.g., "The newest way to lose weight is to give me your money." Problem with use: If the other person doesn't trust new-fangled ideas, you are in trouble. Best to use Ad Antiquitam.

ARGUMENTUM AD NUMERAM:

Meaning: The more people who believe something, the truer it is; e.g., "Most people think I should have the money in your wallet right now." Problem with use: You may need to justify how many people you've surveyed for this request.

ARGUMENTUM AD POPULUM:

Meaning: The people are always right; e.g., "Nine out of 10 people think you should give me your wallet." Problem with use: Far-fetched but could work if you have statistics at hand.

ARGUMENTUM AD VERECUNDIAM:

Meaning: Getting an informed opinion and saying that that opinion is always right; e.g., "Most doctors would agree that the contents of your wallet are too heavy, so you should give me your cash on medical grounds." Problem with use: Works pretty well, actually. Most people are sheep when it comes to authority. ✤◗

KANISZA TRIANGLE ILLUSION

What triangle? The human eye is expert at filling in missing information.

ANIMAL LIES OR TRUTH #1

Lie: The killer whale is psychotic.
Truth: It got its reputation from being a ruthlessly efficient hunter, and mis-readings of *Moby Dick*.

Lie: Dolphins "escort" ships because they crave human company.
Truth: They are surfing either the pressure waves in front of the moving vessel or the bow waves, in order to conserve energy while swimming.

Lie: Goats can't climb trees.
Truth: Actually, in deserts they can and do.

Lie: You can escape from a grizzly bear if it's running at you.
Truth: You cannot. Grizzlies can run, swim, and climb trees faster than you can.

Lie: A camel's hump is full of water.
Truth: It's full of fat that has been laid down from surplus food and will be slowly metabolized for energy. Why a camel can go so long between water holes is because it can metabolize water from this stored fat.

Lie: A cow invented television.

Truth: A cow was used as the antenna for the first television in Scotland.

Lie: Hamsters are placid, to the point of being boring.
Truth: In the wild, hamsters are particularly aggressive in their behavior toward each other and toward any perceived predator. Try snarling at one, but watch out for its razor-sharp teeth. 🖫

ELVIS COULD HAVE BEEN DEFIANT

Tony Curtis and Sidney Poitier were nominated for Oscars for their performances in *The Defiant Ones* in 1958, but they weren't the first choices for the roles. Director Stanley Kramer wanted Elvis Presley and Sammy Davis Jr., who were good friends, to play the parts and both men were keen—especially Elvis, who wanted to do some "proper" acting. But Colonel Tom Parker nixed the notion, maintaining it would damage the King's fan base if they had to watch him getting chummy with a black guy. 🖫

FOOD LIES #1

Hot dogs—While they may be hot, there is (usually) not a trace of dog in a hot dog. Unless, of course, the hot dog you are eating comes from Korea where it is typical to eat dog. So, unless you are eating a Korean hot dog, you are quite probably not eating dog of any sort. You may be eating porklips, horselips, or cowlips.

Hamburgers—There's no ham in a hamburger. Hamburger, as a thing to eat, comes from the German town of Hamburg where, according to legend, it was invented by a merchant who took pounded beef and shaped it into patties for those who could not afford more expensive cuts of meat. Germans brought the "Hamburg steak" with them to America where it became popular. Eventually, the wholesome hamburger, once said to be inspired by the Tartar horseman who tenderized their meat under their saddles, would include mechanically reclaimed meat—bits of animal protein syphoned off the bone.

Toad in the Hole—Despite its frightening and downright upsetting name to all who love *The Wind in the Willows*, there is no toad in this dish. Toad in the Hole was invented by a young English woman whose name has been lost to history. The valiant mom tried to cure her child's fear of toads by renaming the child's favorite dish, sausages in a Yorkshire pudding batter, as Toad in the Hole. The child never got over her fear of toads but the oddly named dish soon became a family favorite.

Bombay Duck—There's no duck in this dish. Rather, the "duck" is a small edible fish from Asia that has a slender, almost transparent body. When dried, this fish is eaten as a side dish to curry. The fish, also called bummalo, has a curious odor which is an acquired pleasure. The name comes from the time of the British Raj when the smell of the fish in the sun recalled the smell of the Bombay Mail train—quite musty and strong. The Hindi word for mail is "dak," hence Bummalo Dak, which soon became bastardized into Bombay Duck. 💾

TROMPE L'OEIL

Trompe l'oeil, or the art of deceiving the eye by painting a three-dimensional form on a two-dimensional surface, is generally used just for decorative effect. However, because of the novel and often amusing effect that a trompe l'oeil can have on unsuspecting viewers, it is an artistic device that can be—and has been—used for nefarious ends by unscrupulous, if talented, artists over the passage of time. That said, if used to deceive, whether intentionally or not, it can get the artist into trouble.

An artform that has been around for a long time, the aim with trompe l'oeil is to produce an image that is indistinguishable from the real thing.

Once upon a time, two highly skilled artists in ancient Greece were vying with each other to see who was the most talented. According to the story told by the 16th-century art historian Vasari, they each submitted a painting in competition. Zeuxis produced a magnificent still life, which featured grapes that were so lifelike that a bird flew down to peck at one. Not a bad result. However, Zeuxis unwittingly and by implication admitted defeat when he turned to his rival Parrhasius and asked him to draw back the curtain in front of his own painting in order to reveal its subject in its entirety. The curtain was itself part of the painting.

Rembrandt's students are reputed to have played a cruel joke on the great master when they painted some highly realistic gold coins on the floor of his studio. The great master was forever poor and much in need of funds, and so his pupils hoped to trick him into scrabbling around on hands and knees trying to pick them up.

William Harnett was a skilled painter who worked in America in the mid to late 1800s. Famous for his paintings of musical instruments and game (rabbits, pheasant, etc.), they were so realistic that when hung on a wall people were fooled into trying to pick them up.

When Harnett began painting dollar bills, however, he got into real trouble. Harnett's paintings of banknotes were brilliantly executed and indistinguishable from the real thing, right down to their creases and worn edges. So realistic were they that in 1887, New York law officers seized a 5-dollar bill, or rather Harnett's painting of a 5-dollar bill, from the wall of a saloon where it hung and demanded that the artist hand over any similar paintings.

When the offending picture was brought before the judge, he said "the development and exercise of a talent so capable of mischief should not be encouraged."

Eager of course to remain on the right side of the law, Harnett never painted money again. ✎

LIES COUPLES TELL #1

As with the Lies Women Tell Men, the course of human relationships and particularly those involving love, rarely run true. The following are examples of some of the lies that men and women tell each other when they're in love.

※ ※ ※

"I was getting up anyway . . ."—There comes a time in every relationship when you realize that telling the truth isn't going to work. Maybe it never did work in the first place. And, because two people are always two people no matter how closely attuned their hearts are, it doesn't pay to tell the truth about getting out of bed/off the sofa/out of meditation/out of your hospital bed. The truth here is: "I really wanted to relax here. But I can't. Because I married *you*." Falling in love means never ever being able to sit and relax as in the days of yore, eating ice cream and pizza idly on the sofa. Now, you have to get up and do something. It's all their fault.

※ ※ ※

"I think we're getting along fine."—Diplomacy rules good relationships. A wise partner recalls that the truth, as they see it, is only their opinion in real terms. So, when someone—anyone—asks how you and your other half are doing, lie. Lie always. No one wants to hear the day-to-day struggles of staying together, least of all your partner. In essence, this little lie could be worse: you have yet to sell the other one into the slave trade nor have either of you put tons of salt in the other one's food. So, in that homey, everyday way, you *are* getting along fine. And if he or she asks, you are *definitely* getting along fine. And if your relationship counselor asks, you've never got along *better*.

※ ※ ※

"I'll never mention it again."—No, the problem will burn with me in hell. There are times when partners fight a losing battle. This stems from the inability to see the other person as a separate entity, with likes and opinions different from your own, i.e., totally wrong. Sometimes it is possible to get them to see your point of view, to make them see common sense. Sometimes, it is not. Knowing what to harangue about and what to let go is, perhaps, the largest part of partner wisdom. Saying that you will never talk about something again, however, is a definite sign that this issue is a bad one. Any partner, upon hearing this, should say to themselves, "Oh s***. I'm in trouble now." ✿

DIRTY TRICKS OF THE WINE TRADE #1

A very bountiful year is not a good thing for a winemaker. Because it is important not to exhaust the soil, in such circumstances the law says that only a certain proportion of the grape crop can be harvested.

In order to do this, the winemaker has to employ the practice of *triage*, whereby he first selects the grapes that are of least use and cuts them off the vine. They must then be left on the ground to rot. Certain unscrupulous winemakers use the "reject" grapes, though, giving the second wine another name so as not to be caught out. Because, inevitably, this wine will be of inferior quality, he will have to mask the taste by using other tricks.

Wine is fermented in barrels, but for an even stronger oaky or woody flavor woodchips are added. This serves to cover up a multitude of sins and sinfully bad wine. It affects the purity of the wine in other ways too: woodchips often absorb bacteria which can be harmful to the consumer. In this respect, the winemaking process itself is the unscrupulous winemaker's greatest ally and its greatest defense. In order to ferment, barrels must be completely sealed. A health regulator, for instance, checking for the addition of woodchips or other baddies would be disrupting the process. ⧖

THE METHOD

When Johnny Depp was preparing for his role in *What's Eating Gilbert Grape?* he took it so seriously he taught himself illiteracy by forcing his brain to forget how to read and write. ⊟●

ROCK MYTHS EXPLODED

"Mama" Cass Elliot choked on a ham sandwich.
Actually, the coroner's report showed her stomach to have been empty, thus she was probably feeling hungry.

Elvis is still alive.
He's not. Really.

The Monkees didn't play or sing on any of their records.
Not in the beginning maybe, but they did as their career went on.

Bob Marley was the first choice for the role of Ivan (the lead character played by Jimmy Cliff) in *The Harder They Come.*
Actually, post-*THTC*, Jimmy Cliff was the first choice for a reggae singer to receive the full rock-star packaging treatment from Island Records, but he wasn't interested so they spent the money on Bob Marley and the *Catch a Fire* album instead.

Donna Summer was once a Sunset Strip hooker.
The closest she got to a life of vice was friendly conversation with the girls who plied their trade outside her record company's offices on L.A.'s Sunset Strip.

Bob Marley witnessed the gangland-style execution of the 4 men who shot him.
While it's true that he attended an impromptu street justice court whereby three of the guilty were condemned to death, he declined any involvement and departed before 2 were shot and 1 hanged from a tree. ⊟

JUSTIN TIMBERLAKE LOST HIS HAIR YEARS AGO

The singing hearthrob owns 27 different wigs, and he is so rich that he has people growing hair for him so he can change his wigs to keep up with all the current trends. Realistic, aren't they? ⊟●

12 AMAZING ANIMAL FACTS

Ducks tell really good jokes. You have to be another duck to get them.

Chimpanzees smile at you because they are pleased to see you.

Apart from humans, meerkats are the only animals in the world that tell lies.

Seals have no gender, and during the mating season when they pair off, they spend a long time arguing over who's the daddy.

The horse is an endangered species.

Fish know what you are thinking.

Bears like porridge.

The macaroni penguin likes cheese.

If a flamingo lifts up the other leg it will fall over.

Reindeer can fly.

A gnu will advise you on anything.

Buffalo aren't extinct, they're just in hiding. 📖🎖

THE PRESIDENT'S LIES

RICHARD M. NIXON

I am not a crook.
The president states his innocence, 1974.

I can say categorically that this investigation indicates that no one in the White House staff, no one in this administration, presently employed, was involved in this very bizarre incident.
The president refers to an inquiry into the Watergate break-in that was being conducted at his request by presidential counsel John Dean. It was news to Dean at the time, though, who

not only had not made any investigation, but hadn't met with the president to discuss an inquiry, either.

What really hurts in matters of this sort is not the fact that they occur, because overzealous people in campaigns do things that are wrong. What hurts is if you try to cover it up.
The president on the Watergate affair. The cover-up of the break-in on Democratic Party offices – which happened on 17 June 1972—began the morning of 18 June. 📖

HARRY BENSON: 19TH-CENTURY SWINDLER EXTRAORDINAIRE

Harry Benson was born into an afflu-ent Jewish family in Paris. He had a charming, erudite, aristocratic manner, and spoke several languages. His packed career—he was only just over 40 when he died—began in the early 1870s when, posing as "The Compte de Montague, Mayor of Châteaudun" he managed to extract £1,000 from the Mayor of London which, he claimed, would be used to help victims of the Franco-Prussian War. He was found out and sent to prison, where he attempted to burn himself to death, but only suc-ceeded in crippling himself to the extent that he needed crutches for the rest of his life.

Back on the outside, his brief flirta-tion with going straight—advertising himself as a potential secretary able to speak several languages—came to an abrupt end when his advertisement was answered by William Kurr, a turf

swindler. Kurr's crude method of reliev-ing customers of their money was to run off with their winnings. Benson convinced Kurr that there were far more sophisticated, and lucrative, ways of extorting money from the racing fraternity.

Together the two of them set up a free magazine for circulation among the French aristocracy. Entitled *Le Sport*, it contained articles about rac-ing culled from British newspapers and translated, and introduced its readers to a mythical character called G. H. Yonge. This man, claimed *Le Sport*, had had such success backing horses that bookmakers in Britain would not deal with him without making their odds less favorable.

Benson's longer game was soon pay-ing off. The Comtesse de Goncourt received a letter from the famous Mr. Yonge asking her whether she would act as an intermediary in the placing of his bets. He would send her a check, he said, and all she had to do was send it to a particular bookmaker's—another of Harry Benson's aliases, of course—and place it on the horse he told her to. If it won, then she would forward the money on to Mr. Yonge and receive a 5 percent commission.

This the Comtesse did on a number of occasions, placing "bets" of a few hundred pounds on his behalf, receiving "winnings" of several hundred more, and earning herself a tidy little "fee" in the process. As all the best swindlers do, Benson had won her trust. Stage 1 of the master plan was completed. Sure enough, in time, the Comtesse offered this fantastically successful bettor £10,000 of her own money. She never saw it again.

Benson and Kurr then departed from the world of racing bound for their next great adventure. This involved "taming" three senior Scotland Yard policemen one by one. Eventually Chief Inspector John Meiklejohn, Chief Inspector Nathanial Druscovich, and Chief Inspector William Palmer were all supplementing their incomes by accepting payment for keeping quiet about the activities of Benson and Kurr.

But those activities came to an end for a while when, in a rare lapse of judgment, Benson approached the Comtesse for more money. The Comtesse's lawyer checked out Mr. Yonge by contacting Scotland Yard. Benson and Kurr were protected and kept abreast of things there, but Parisian police too were beginning to apply pressure to Scotland Yard to make some arrests of people who were clearly extorting money.

Eventually the whole affair unraveled and all concerned went to prison. Benson and Kurr, having served 15 and 10 years respectively, continued swindling together on their release. First, ever with an eye to the current opportunity for making a quick, easy buck, they went to the U.S. and acted as mining company promoters there. Then Benson traveled to Belgium, where he proceeded to sell stock in mines that did not exist. He was caught out, jailed for 2 years, and on release moved to Switzerland.

While there, posing as a stockbroker, he asked a young woman to marry him. He also asked her father to invest £7,000 in an investment project. Benson tried to flee with the money but the father managed to send the police after him and he was caught. He returned £5,000 to the father who decided not to prosecute.

Benson's final, unsuccessful con ended when he was caught trying to sell bogus Adelina Patti tickets in the U.S. Poor old Harry, unable to bear the idea of another stretch in prison, jumped from a tall building to his death. At least, that's what was reported. ⌛

LIES ABOUT WRITING

There are a series of supposedly concrete rules that aspiring authors should follow, in order to help them make the most of their talents. Most of these "rules" take the form of friendly advice on what or who to write about. People who offer such advice are invariably lying in order to fend off unwanted competition.

"Write about what you know."—A lie: no one wants to know what you know unless you've come back from the dead. If you are going to write, write about something none of us knows—how the inside of a woman's head works, how to talk to men, how to make a billion dollars, how to make our mothers happy without sacrificing our lifestyles, how to talk to our fathers. We don't want to know how you got through your day at the office.

"If you can talk, you can write."—Another lie: if you can talk, then you can talk. Writing is very close to not talking. There are no sounds. There is no one to talk to. You are, if anything, talking to yourself. And, as anyone who has sat next to someone who was talking to themselves knows, that isn't exciting or interesting. Writing is not like talking. Only dialog is like talking.

"It's not about what you know, but who you know."—A lie: it certainly helps to know something. If you know how to do something interesting or amusing, then your writing is of more value to people than a bad book well marketed because the writer knows someone useful. It is an outright lie that you can know nothing and write a good book—just as it is true that getting a book out there without knowing someone helpful can be a tough row to hoe.

"It only takes one hit book to have a career."—A total lie, as many one-hit wonders can tell you. One hit means you didn't have the courage to get out there and create another hit. You've only got one book in you. That doesn't mean you are a writer. It means you are an author. Once. The publishing and book-buying world is just as trend driven as any other marketplace. What this means is that unless you write a classic that can be updated every year, you'll be about as welcome as day-old bread.

"This isn't autobiographical."—Another complete lie. There is a tendency for main characters to have similar opinions, mannerisms, and even politics as the authors who created them. Everything writers write about is autobiographical out of necessity. They are the experiencer, they are the writer, they are the observer. How could what they write not be filtered through their eyes?

"I never base characters on people I know."—An out-and-out lie. Authors have to base characters on people they know, or at least parts of people they know. As philosophers have pointed out, one has to have real information for the imagination to work on. Therefore, even a "fictional" character would be comprised of elements that factual people had. Any author who says this is lying and knows it. No one could come up with a character with no actual basis in reality, not a believable one anyway.

"Never give up."—Another lie. Many would-be writers and authors should give up trying to write professionally. This is true of any job. If you are lousy at it and it makes you miserable, you probably shouldn't be doing it at all. Especially with writing, singing, acting, dancing, and other high-profile creative employment. On the other hand, if you can't *not* write, this is not a lie. The lie is that determination and nothing else will get you published. It will not. Talent, luck, and hanging out with other writers is the way to go.

"Make every word count."—Thomas Jefferson once said that if you can write the same meaning with one word rather than several you should opt for the one. That idea pales when one considers that the average novel has to be at least 100,000 words long; many are far over that. It is inconceivable that all of those words have to be there for the meaning and impact of the book to work. Every word doesn't need to count. It just needs to be counted.

"Write better for yourself, not other writers."—A lie. You must write for the market, write for your readers, and write for yourself. You must also write better, more distinctively, and with more notoriety than other writers with whom you are competing. You're not only competing with them for readers, but for shelf space and money. This is a highly structured, hotly contested industry, not a self-help conference for one.

"Make sure your story has a beginning, a middle, and an end."—Another lie. If it doesn't ever have an end—and it gets published—you can carry on and on until the character or you grow old and die. Having a well-structured book only means that the sequel will be harder to write and hence the movie rights less attractive. ✿

LIE DETECTORS

The polygraph, as the lie detector is more correctly known ("poly" means many, alluding to the multiple nature of the physical reactions monitored), has been with us now for nearly 100 years. It was invented in 1915 by William Marston, a Harvard-trained psychologist who, under the pseudonym of Charles Moulton, also created the comic-book character Wonder Woman. The concept behind the polygraph is that the act of lying uncontrollably heightens anxiety and increases physiological stress resulting in sweating, faster heart beat, and higher respiration. The polygraph relies upon picking up these slight involuntary changes at specific times in response to a question, and are noted as "spikes" on a graph.

The subject is wired up to the machine with a blood pressure cuff wrapped around the arm, tubes around the chest and abdomen to record the respiratory rate, and sensors on the fingertips to record perspiration. A typical session takes around 2 hours and involves just 2 people, the subject and interviewer. The interviewer spends some time chatting to the subject initially, to put them at ease and monitor their normal physical reactions. Test questions are asked to help the interviewer calibrate the polygraph. A "guilty" reading from one of the physical reactions cannot be taken as proof, but an experienced operator should, so polygraph defenders say, be able to make an informed judgment about whether someone is telling the truth when taking the results as a whole.

The biggest problem with polygraphs is that the body reacts in the same way to a whole range of different emotions, from fear and anger to embarrassment, which is why results are usually inadmissible in a U.S. court of law (although it is admissible in the state of New Mexico). However, the polygraph is used by the military and law enforcement agencies and for employment screening for government jobs and in the private sector. In the U.S., there are well over 3,000 registered polygraph operators or forensic psychophysiologists, some 2,000 of whom belong to professional organizations. 📖

SELLING LIES #1

Ever since man decided that the best way to live was in a capitalist society where everything has its price and everything can be bought and sold, men have excelled in the art of selling. In this, our age of the eternal selling, men can now sell to us "virtually" and with such subtlety that we can often not notice that we've purchased something until the check for it arrives. Here are some of the seller's greatest lies. If you hear or read these words, beware.

❋   ❋   ❋

"Trust me."—Caveat Emptor—let the buyer beware—has been around since Roman times for very good reason. No matter how charismatic, charming, or reasonable your seller may be, if you're a buyer, you cannot trust them. "Trust me" is perhaps the most usual phrase employed by salespeople to get the buyer to put their discernment away. Anyone who promises to take you through a gauntlet of paperwork or details without you reading and understanding all of it is trying to fleece you. While they may not be lying when they ask you to trust them, they are willingly leading you astray. Even if a salesperson doesn't work on commission, there is usually something in the way they sell you, say, a car that will net them a profit. Other gags such as "This is our cost price" and "I have to clear this with my manager" are all sales hogwash. The real price is one you'll never see—unless you end up in court.

❋   ❋   ❋

"This is the last one available." —Unless China has gone bust, this is never true. There will always be another thing you wanted, perhaps just not at that store. Don't buy anything that is the last one unless it is massively discounted and you know the other prices it has been marked at. The last one may be a return, damaged, repaired, or reconditioned. Also, it may not be returnable if something is wrong with it.

❋   ❋   ❋

"I'll throw this in for free."—Nothing is ever free. You pay for it somewhere along the line. While a salesperson is being polite when they say such things, don't be a sucker. They've given this deal to every other customer who has been in the market for what you're buying. You are not special to any salesman— unless you're married to them. (Being a close relative often does not count for much.) ❀

RABBIT/DUCK ILLUSION

HERMAN GRID ILLUSION

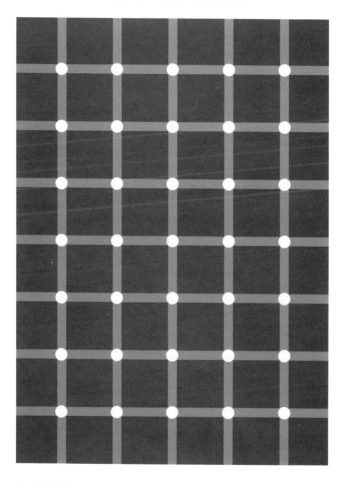

Are the circles between the squares black or white? Well, it depends . . .

A TOOTH LEFT IN A GLASS OF COKE OVERNIGHT WILL DISSOLVE

Not so. This myth is often used in an attempt to put children off the delights of Coca-Cola. According to author Frederick Allen in his 1995 book about Coke, *Secret Formula*, it probably originated from research done by Professor Clive M. McCay of Cornell University in the 1950s. McCay claimed that after two days, a tooth left in a glass of Coca-Cola would become soft and begin to dissolve.

But, chemists went on to explain, anything containing sugar and phosphoric acid would do so after a period of time, and we are helped by the fact that we do not soak our teeth in such substances continuously for days on end, and that our saliva helps to neutralize the potentially damaging acid. ☒

ADVERTISING LIES

Sentences that will sell you anything, if you're dumb enough to believe them.

"FUN FOR THE WHOLE FAMILY."
Nothing is fun for the whole family. If anything, this claim guarantees that no one in the family will enjoy what is on offer. Even at its best, anything that regards itself as wholesome family fun will appeal to one family member—and it will be that member who either stays home, sits in the car and won't come out, or is dead. Family fun can only happen when every family member gets to do exactly what they want to do: get away from the other family members.

"SOMETHING FOR EVERYONE."
The only thing any single shop can offer is that they will have something for no one. No business can cater to every segment of the population. But that doesn't stop store managers all over America luring innocent shoppers to their lair with the promise that there will indeed be something for them.

"THE BEST KEPT SECRET IN TOWN."
No, it isn't the best-kept secret in town. It is not even a secret. ✽

SELLING THE EIFFEL TOWER

Originally erected in 1889 for the Paris Exhibition, amazingly you would think, the Eiffel Tower was never intended to become permanent. By the 1920s the city authorities had decided that they could no longer afford the upkeep of the tower and would scrap it. At least, that was a story floated in a Parisian newspaper at the time.

Inspired by such an article complaining about how costly the tower was to keep in good repair and how it was thus falling into disrepair, Victor Lustig, a conman from Czechoslovakia, devised a cunning plan. Swinging into action, he had some government stationery forged and, posing as a government official, sent out invitations to several scrap-metal merchants in France inviting them to a meeting at the very smart Hotel Crillon on the Place de la Concorde.

At the meeting, Lustig presented himself as a representative of the Ministry of Posts and Telegraphs explaining that he had been charged with arranging for the scrapping of the tower, such was the expense of its upkeep, and was inviting bids from the merchants. However, due to the fact that this would provoke a public outcry as by now the tower had become such a landmark, the meeting had to be kept highly confidential.

At the meeting Lustig identified his "mark" as being Andre Poisson.

Reinforcing the need for secrecy, Lustig took him to one side and confided that, as a government official, he was expected to look and live the part by dressing well and entertaining on a grand scale, but all on a small pittance of a salary. Poisson realized that Lustig was looking for a bribe, and assuming that he was just another corrupt official, duly paid up, in addition to giving him the agreed sum for the tower. With a suitcase full of francs, Lustig boarded a train for Austria where he set about spending his ill-gotten gains. Scanning the press daily for news of the scam he was initially puzzled by the lack of reports, but soon concluded that Poisson must have uncovered the scam but was too embarrassed to go to the police. So, Lustig returned to Paris to do it all over again. However, this time the dealer informed the police. Lustig managed to avoid arrest but the whole thing blew up in the newspapers and he had to exit, pronto, for the United States.

Lustig continued plying his trade as a career conman in the U.S., but was arrested in 1934 for his involvement in counterfeiting dollar bills. Dispatched to jail, he made a storybook escape by climbing down a rope made of torn sheets but was recaptured 27 days later in Pittsburgh, Pennsylvania. This time he was sent to Alcatraz where he died in 1947 of pneumonia. 🖎

DIET LIES #1

EAT WHATEVER YOU USUALLY EAT BUT ONLY EAT HALF OF IT:
If you can. Pushing the plate away—or being aware of whether you really are
satiated or not—isn't as easy as it sounds. If one could actually train oneself to
eat half or even two-thirds of what they normally eat while keeping or adding
more activity into their day, this diet tip would work. The trouble is getting
hungry. If you were trapped in a cell where you were only fed half of your
normal allotment, you would lose weight. However, most of us are not in a cell.
We're standing in a line at our nearest Dunkin' Donuts.

NO DIET WORKS. YOU'RE EITHER FAT FOR GOOD OR NOT:
There is some truth in the idea that people have a "set point" for their weight—
that is, there is a weight for them that is easy to maintain. In Western society,
with its culture of snacking on empty calories and an overabundance of available
foodstuffs, this "set point" is often overweight. Further research has shown,
however, that *any* diet works fairly well if it is actually adhered to. Seeing as most
diets advise eating less, taking more care with one's food and its preparation, and
taking more exercise, it is hard to see how they may fail. It is the human part of
the equation which lets the side down, not the theory or the plan.

NERVOUS PEOPLE BURN OFF MORE CALORIES:
In a recent study, it was suggested that nervous people—those who fidget a lot,
tap their toes, drum on the desk, etc.—tend to burn off more calories than the
laid-back, easy-going brownie munchers who loaf in the corner of the room. The
downside of being nervous is that fidgety activity can also cause undue nibbling
of high-calorie foods, especially if being nervous links with social situations that
involve alcohol. The notion of comfort eating—eating food to quell an upset—
can often apply to those who are uncomfortable without food-supplied
distractions. There are fat nervous people just as there are thin, calm folks. 🖫

BEATING THE POLYGRAPH

Professional criminals and others wanting to put this computerized bloodhound off the scent mask their involuntary test reactions with stronger reactions that override them:

Bite your tongue, or push a sharp tack through the sole of your shoe and press down on it before you answer every question. This causes a painful reaction, which can override the involuntary "spike" and make the reaction consistent throughout.

Apply a strong antiperspirant to the fingertips to stop perspiration.

Taking a sedative before a polygraph session dulls emotions and reactions.

Ratchet up your emotional response rather than trying to conceal your emotions.

Thinking of something extremely unpleasant or painful before every question can also skew the results. 📖

IS IT A BOY OR IS IT A GIRL?

Sarah (Emma) Edmonds was a patriotic Canadian who decided to swap genders early on in life in order to escape her authoritarian father. She left home and made her way to Michigan in the U.S. where she first worked selling Bibles. When the Civil War broke out she answered the call for the Union Army and tried to enlist. Calling herself Frank Thompson, she finally succeeded on the fourth attempt and was taken on as a male nurse. She volunteered for spying duties and crossed into enemy lines a total of 11 times, assuming different disguises, sometimes even as a negro field hand, both male and female.

But living a lie eventually took its toll and "Frank" became ill with malaria. Realizing that her identity would soon be revealed if she was admitted to the hospital, Sarah entered the ranks of deserters and reverted to her own gender, working as a nurse in Washington D.C. until the end of the war. She married in 1867 and had 3 sons, one of whom entered the military, "just like Mamma." ✄

LOVE CHEAT LIES #2

While this book will give examples of the lies that men tell women and women tell men and are specific to each sex, in the interests of fairness it seems appropriate that we also offer you advice on some lies that are unisex. Because we live in a time of greater sexual equality than ever before, the old ideas of only men being able to "work late" and therefore cover their tracks is long gone. Now women "work late" too. They also own cell phones.

"MY CELL HAD NO SIGNAL/BATTERY RAN OUT."

With more and better coverage and with improved battery life and maintenance, these excuses will be something of the past, as anachronistic as one's horse going lame. Granted, there are times when it could be possible that your maybe-cheating spouse so-happened not to be in an area where there was adequate cell signal (in a nuclear bunker, for example). And it is possible, certainly, that a phone that was supposed to be charged wasn't. As cell phones are, for many of us, a lifeline to the world, anyone who doesn't check their battery supply before heading out is fairly foolish. Neither of these are acceptable excuses really, unless at the first opportunity to call you, they do so. They must mention the signal/battery thing right away too. Or else something smells funny in Denmark.

"I RAN INTO JILL. YOU REMEMBER, I USED TO WORK WITH HER."

Uh, no you don't, actually. But the fact that it is a woman or someone who your partner knew beforehand isn't good. Lingering passions can burn for years and if someone comes free, it can open up a world of sexual opportunity. Old workmates, ex-lovers, almost lovers, roommates' old friends, friends of the family, someone they spent time with at camp and, of course, old classmates are all categories of suspicious new people. The fact that you may not remember Jill could well mean that she doesn't know about you and that your partner is spoken for. Other forms of this excuse are "I ran into [X] after work and we decided to catch up . . ." when your partner isn't the sort of person who stops off to catch up with people they never spoke about in all your time together. A natural event would be bumping into an old friend, exchanging contact details, and then making a date in the future to catch up. Unless they are in an airport or warzone, this is not an acceptable excuse. Your cheater-detection bells should be ringing in your ears.

"BOWLING NIGHT TONIGHT, SORRY."

But he doesn't bowl. Or he never bowled until a month ago. Or no one told you that he took up bowling. Or he owns no bowling paraphernalia. In fact, he doesn't even dress properly to go bowling. He wears aftershave and brushes his teeth to go bowling. He never asks you to come along to the alley with him. He hates all kinds of sport. He doesn't know the first thing about bowling or scoring or how to throw the ball. He doesn't say anything about the rental shoes or the other balls the guys are using. In fact, it doesn't seem that he knows anything about bowling except for the fact that this night is his bowling night and you're not invited.

"I RAN OUT OF GAS, BELIEVE IT OR NOT."

People can run out of gas. They can miss trains, planes, and boats. People can forget something and have to go back to work to get it. All sorts of things can happen but they rarely do without a warning phone call or a breathless excuse. Not that you would ask to see the receipt for the gas that she or he bought after they ran out. Not that you would ask to sniff their hands for the telltale, lingering whiff of unleaded gasoline. Not that you would enquire how many miles were on the odometer and how many miles to the gallon you think that car is getting. Running out of gas happens but usually to those who have no money or have made a bad judgment on distances.

"OH, THAT CALL? IT WAS [X] FROM WORK . . ."

Mysterious phone calls mean three things: it is your birthday, there's something going on that he or she doesn't want to share with you (usually work or family or finance), or they are cheating on you and being really sloppy about it. Most cell phones will display the caller's number before one picks up the call. Also, unless it is set otherwise, most cell phones have a caller return facility, which, if you dared, you could insist your partner use. "Oh," you could say, "Call X back! I want to ask them something." If your partner refuses, then be assured there is something fishy going on. Phone calls taken in the other room, spoken in hushed tones or extremely brief answers, are a sure sign of sneakiness. Over-acting and eye-histrionics are another sign of nervous, get-it-over-quick cheating phone calls.❀

OF COURSE YOU'RE FIRST CHOICE . . .

Possibly the greatest lie told to actors in Hollywood by directors, producers, and studios. Superstar actors have supersensitive egos and once they've signed up for a role, they want to believe that they were the one and only choice for it.

Arnold Schwarzenegger was first choice for the lead in the *The Terminator*?
In fact, Director James Cameron favored an actor called Lance Henriksen, but the producers wanted somebody their audience might have heard of, so the dialog was scaled back and Arnie got the job.

Robert DeNiro was the first choice to play Al Capone in Brian DePalma's 1987 movie *The Untouchables*?
Actually, Bob Hoskins was signed up and went so far as to start rehearsing the role, then DeNiro "became available" and the vertically-challenged Englishman was sent on his way with a $200,000 pay-off for a couple of weeks' work.

John Voight and Burt Reynolds were the first-choice actors for *Deliverance*?
Their roles were originally offered to and turned down by Henry Fonda and Marlon Brando respectively, because they felt the parts were too physically dangerous.

Christopher Reeve was the first choice to play Superman?
Not even the second or third choice: Nick Nolte, Warren Beatty, and Robert Redford were all "unavailable."

King Charles was the first choice to play National Velvet?
Actually, that wasn't a lie. The 7-year-old Thoroughbred was picked by the then 11-year-old Elizabeth Taylor and became the real star of the 1944 movie.

STAN LAUREL WAS THE STUPID ONE

Actually, it was Stan who would work out the duo's sight gags and stunts, going over them with the directors, cameraman, and technicians, while Ollie was off playing golf. 💾

THE BEST HUMAN LIE DETECTORS

The most successful human lie detectors are people with a rare medical condition called Wernicke's aphasia. it is a type of damage in the left hemisphere of the brain that makes them unable properly to understand language. In a 2000 study published in *Nature* magazine, aphasics were found to be 73 percent successful at telling when someone was lying, perhaps because they read microcosmic facial expressions rather than concentrating on what a person is saying. A significant percentage of left-handers also use their right-brain to process visual, non-linguistic functions and tend to be better at detecting lies than right-handed people.

Some FBI agents were found in one study to be better at detecting lies than the average person. They are trained in a linguistic technique called statement analysis, in which they analyse a witness's written statement, looking for deviations from the normal context. They look for people talking about a missing person in the past tense or always saying "my husband and I" instead of "we" (in a spousal murder case, it denotes separation and the use of a lot of negative emotional language suggests lying, to give them topics to focus on in future interrogations).

A 2004 California study found that, out of a test sample of 13,000 people, only 31 were excellent judges of when someone was lying, being right most of the time. It seems that the ability to tell whether someone is lying relies more on the ability to read their micro-facial expressions and tiny body language cues than on the ability to decipher what they say. ✿

PLAY IT AGAIN SAM

It's *Casablanca*'s most quoted line but it's never heard in the movie. What Humphrey Bogart really said to Dooley Wilson was, "You played it for her now play it for me. Play it!" 💾

STRANGER IN A STRANGE LAND

Three hundred years ago London was a vibrant and cosmopolitan city, just as it is today. Its inhabitants were accustomed to seeing foreigners among them. But in 1703, visitors from Formosa, now known as Taiwan, were at the very least a rarity and more than likely completely unknown. It was in this particular year that a young Formosan gentleman in his 20s first entered the city via a somewhat roundabout route.

Scottish clergyman William Innes had first met George Psalmanazar in Holland. George claimed to be a Latin-speaking Japanese, but when Innes asked him to translate a piece of Cicero into Japanese, George faltered. He could certainly manage the Latin, but the Japanese stumped him.

Spotting the PR possibilities of making a swift guinea or two, and despite being a man of the cloth, Innes suggested George change his purported country of origin to somewhere a little more exotic and unfamiliar—Formosa fit the bill nicely.

Duly equipped with an interesting new nationality, George was taken to London by Innes and quickly became famous as the must-have guest at all the best people's society events.

Making the most of his new-found celebrity status, George decided to write an account of his homeland, and *An Historical and Geographical Description of Formosa* was an instant success. Written in Latin and translated into English, it was also translated into French and German. Pandering to a public just as eager for shlock-horror stories as it is today, the book reported on some very grisly practices—cannibalism and burning of the hearts of some 20,000 young boys in order to appease the gods.

Murderers were apparently hung upside down and used as target practice for would be Robin Hoods, while lesser criminals merely had their arms

and legs cut off. To this bloodbath was added a tantalizing hint of sexual excess, as polygamy was also endorsed wholeheartedly. George illustrated the book with drawings of buildings, costumes and religious artifacts, and even went so far as to give a detailed breakdown of the Formosan alphabet.

Despite George's distinctly unoriental appearance (blond hair, pale skin, and round eyes), a great many people bought into the story enthusiastically, until doubts began to be raised by those who had been to Asia and knew that, generally speaking, oriental peoples do not share the caucasian looks common in Europe. In 1706 George confessed that it had all been a pack of lies.

He became a reformed and extremely pious character, vehemently regretting his youthful prank. He made a career as a man of letters and was even befriended by Samuel Johnson. Although he lived into his 80s and published his memoirs posthumously, George never admitted his true origins. He is thought to have been French. ✎

JAMES CAAN'S BUM RAP

The rumors are that James Caan disappeared in the 1980s because his volatile temper and pharmaceutical recreational tendencies meant nobody was prepared to work with him. Actually, he couldn't get work because his off-screen hobbies—rodeo riding, motorbike and powerboat racing, and karate—meant no completion bond company (firms that insure films against not being finished or going over budget) would handle a movie with him in it. ▣

NEW AGE LIES #2

IT'S NOT THAT GOD OR THE UNIVERSE IS LYING TO YOU, BUT . . .

There are among us people who have discovered a form of spirituality and peace that does not come from the old, organized religions, but from something called New Age teachers. Horribly, somehow New Age teachings have become common practice among otherwise normal-seeming people. Sadly, these people are forever attempting to pass on their "wisdom" to the unenlightened among us. So, whenever you are faced with a New Age disciple trying to "convert" you to their way of thinking, answer their lies thus:

❊ ❊ ❊

"I am at peace with the universe"—That's good because the universe really hated you being mad at it. This is a lie as well: actually you are extremely angry with the universe for not getting the good parking space today and for the spilling of the fresh coffee during the meeting. By lying to yourself, you pretend to be at ease with the way things are. You're not.

❊ ❊ ❊

"I love and accept myself."—This lie is mere words. You love yourself? You accept yourself? Could you be anyone else? Loving and accepting yourself makes perfect sense to anyone who is mentally stable. Hating yourself and not accepting the way you are marks you out as a neurotic who has no friends, no sense of reality, and certainly no boyfriend or girlfriend.

❊ ❊ ❊

"I am unique and loving, loved and free."—And your proof for this is what? You are just as unique as anyone else, really, if you think about it. Unique isn't so important. Loving and loved and free are judgments that you probably aren't in a position to make with any sense of validity.

❊ ❊ ❊

"I am safe and always feel protected."—This would be true only if you had iron underwear. Life is always dangerous. To think that you are safe and that you have a sense of protection is to coddle yourself in false belief. You are not safe nor will you be. As for those feelings of being protected, you can forget about them too. You will die, as will everyone else.

✖ ✖ ✖

"I trust my inner being to lead me in the right path."—Let's hope my inner being remembers where I parked the car. While this may not be an out-and-out lie, the notion of an inner being that leads you onto the best way of life is a dangerous one. What if your inner being is playful or mischievous? What if you're listening to the man beside you's inner being instead of your own? Better to make your own judgments rather than rely on someone you can't even see.

✖ ✖ ✖

"I am a success in all that I do."—This is only true if you set your standards very low. To be successful in everything you do, you would have to be psychotic. No one can succeed in absolutely everything, nor should they want to. Failure is one of the few ways we learn and it is what other people can sympathize with. So, why lie to yourself and say that everything you do is perfect?

✖ ✖ ✖

"I always spend money wisely."—So how do you explain that gold lamé cardigan? This is a trick statement because what you may consider a wise bargain another person may consider a total waste of resources. The sooner you face the fact that you are a squanderer, just like your father, the better off you will be. You are, yet again, using New Age affirmations to lie to yourself. ✹

THE MYSTIC FOXES

In 1848 in upstate New York, two young sisters, Catherine (Kate) and Margaret Fox, complained to their mother that they could hear tapping noises inside the family home. Their mother couldn't work out what was causing them and called in the neighbors. The story that unseen spirits were at large and communicating with the two young girls quickly spread around the neighborhood. People wanted to see, or rather hear, for themselves and soon elder sister Ann Leah, not blessed with the "gift" herself, began organizing public demonstrations.

From there, it was a short step to ramping up the action and orchestrating staged events on a grander scale. By 1850 demand was such that the sisters traveled to New York City and held séances, during which they communicated with the spirit world. Ann, in the role of manager, began touring the girls in a kind of mystic roadshow. Money changed hands at a fast rate and the séances were soon providing all three women with a decent living. People were fascinated. Invited to ask the spirits questions, an answer would be rapped out in a kind of unearthly Morse code. The séances developed further to include spirit writing and other mystic manifestations. Kate and Margaret would often summon the spirits of the famous but on one occasion, when in touch with Benjamin Franklin, Margaret

left the table in a huff when one of the sitters remarked that the great statesman's grasp of grammar seemed to be surprisingly lacking. Although skeptics tried to catch them out, they were unsuccessful and a great many people were convinced of the authenticity of the Fox girls' performances.

By the time Kate and Margaret began a tour of the U.S., the spiritualist movement had been well and truly born and others claiming to have "the gift" began acting as mediums, conveying messages to and from "the other side." Unfortunately, during the 1860s, fame, the stress of performing, and the realization that they had inadvertently given rise to a new cult took its toll on both sisters and they began to drink heavily. Kate married Englishman Henry D. Jencken on a tour of the U.K., but eventually had their two children taken away from her due to her alcoholism. Ann Leah disassociated herself from her sisters after marrying a wealthy banker.

On 21 October 1888, Margaret shocked the country when she issued a confession in the *New York World*. She said that the whole thing had begun as a prank, "'We were very mischievous children and we wanted to terrify our dear mother." She explained that the sisters had made the noises themselves, principally by cracking their toes and other joints. No one had believed that young children could be capable of such deception and the whole thing had just ballooned from there gaining a momentum of its own. That same night, Margaret repeated her confession in front of a crowd at the New York Academy of Music. But many people simply did not believe her, and sure enough Margaret later retracted the confession. Sadly, the sisters both died penniless within a year of each other, Kate in 1892 and Margaret in 1893. ✎

TOP 12 PROFESSIONAL LIARS

Some people need to be prepared to lie and prevaricate, or at least be "economical with the truth" for professional reasons. Unsurprisingly the jobs that require people who have a flair for telling an untruth convincingly are very well paid. But then, since they may well require the strength to live out a retirement with the kind of support offered by expensive therapy or expensive wines, then large financial recompense would be needed to tempt a person into those professions. Which are:

1. Secret agents and spies
2. Politicians
3. Civil servants
4. Doctors
5. Lawyers
6. Criminals
7. Confidence tricksters
8. Fraudsters
9. Magicians
10. Salespeople
11. Military personnel
12. Fortune-tellers and mediums 📖

THANKS, MOLOTOV

With true hippie logic, the Molotov cocktail, a petrol bomb favored by 1960s street-fighting revolutionaries, was actually named after a man of diplomacy. It was in "honor" of Vyacheslav Mikhailovich Molotov, a Soviet commissar for foreign affairs, who negotiated a non-aggression pact with Germany and was part of the founding conference of the United Nations. 🖬

ALWAYS CARRY I.D.

Short people get drunk quicker than tall people, because there is less of them to be affected by the alcohol. 🖬◆

THE KOMODO DRAGON

It's just a big lizard. 💾

WILLIAM IRELAND—NOT SHAKESPEARE

William Ireland was born in the mid 1770s, son of the Earl of Sandwich's ex-mistress and Samuel Ireland, a late 18th-century architect, author, and painter. The boy's father was not interested in William, thinking him dull and lazy. However Samuel was passionate about Shakespeare. He was a voracious collector of anything to do with his hero, and would spend evenings in their home just off the Strand in London reading the works of Shakespeare to his family.

What Samuel did not appreciate was that his son was also something of a poet. William was fascinated by a story his father had told him of Thomas Chatterton, who had forged poems of 15th-century priest Thomas Rowley. Starved of attention, William decided to see if he could pull off a forgery or two of his own. Samuel was taken in by his son's tentative first two attempts: a dedicatory letter from the

author, which William said he had found in a book which used to belong to Queen Elizabeth I, and a letter from Oliver Cromwell to a high-ranking official named John Bradshaw.

Spurred on by obtaining the approval of his father for the first time, William became more ambitious. When he presented his father with a mortgage deed made between Michael Fraser and his wife, and John Heminge and William Shakespeare, Samuel was ecstatic. So much so, that he gave his son the pick of the books in his library. Samuel was not about to stop there. He had already taken tips on making documents appear old, and spun his father a yarn about having met an eccentric, secretive aristocrat—"Mr. H."—in a coffee house who had a chest full of documents that did not interest him. Potentially this ruse allowed the deception to continue indefinitely.

William wrote more letters from

Shakespeare, which his father's eminent friends declared were the work of a genius. It was clearly time, felt William, to try his hand at some poems and plays. It was looking good. On 15 December 1795, Richard Brinsley Sheridan, the manager of the Drury Lane Theatre, agreed to show the first of these "lost" plays of Shakespeare, *Vortigern and Rowena*, but there were beginning to be rumblings of doubt about the veracity of these newly unearthed documents. Still the play went ahead and for the first two acts the detractors appeared to be silenced.

Then came the third act. One or two of the actors had been miscast, which made the clumsiness of some of the language all the more pronounced. The audience was soon in an uproar. The public had rejected the play. It was the end of *Vortigern* and, William assumed, the end of him. Still refusing to disclose the identity of Mr. H. and feeling unable to tell the truth to his father, he told his sisters the whole story. They passed it on to Samuel, but however much others implored him to look at the facts, his father would not believe that his son was capable of such forgery. Samuel Ireland maintained that the works were those of William Shakespeare until his dying day in 1800. ⧗

JOHN WAYNE PERFORMED ALL HIS OWN STUNTS

That was always the studio PR line, and vociferously backed up by The Duke himself, but Wayne's long term stunt double was a seldom-photographed chap named Chuck Robertson. 💾

EXPLODING HEALTH MYTHS

Despite the massive improvements in medicine over the past century, there persists in our society a number of ridiculous lies told about what affects our health. These include:

SKIPPING MEALS WILL HELP YOU LOSE WEIGHT.

In the (very) long run if you don't eat of course the pounds will fall off, but immediately if you start missing meals your body goes into something called Starvation Mode. In order to make what food you do eat last over those long periods of not eating, your metabolism will slow down and start storing what you are eating as fat.

THREE MEALS A DAY IS WHAT YOU SHOULD BE EATING.

No, the best way to eat to maintain the average healthy metabolism is five small meals a day rather than three (or fewer—see above) larger ones.

YOU CATCH COLD FROM GETTING COLD.

A cold is a virus, and you are more likely to pick one up in a warm, crowded environment where germs thrive. It's called a cold because the symptoms make you shiver and you feel better when you are kept warm.

VEGETARIANISM IS ALWAYS THE HEALTHY OPTION.

It will only work for you as long as you are getting adequate protein from other sources. This is especially true for children who are still growing.

THE CURE FOR BALDNESS.

If your number is called on the male pattern baldness lottery, there is nothing you can do other than accept your fate with good grace and a sense of panache. Absolutely none of the advertised miracle cures work.

BALDNESS SKIPS A GENERATION.

There is, as yet, no scientific explanation or formula for how and why male pattern baldness affects some men and not others and in different ways, thus it seems to be completely random as to who and how it strikes. So don't blame your grandfather. 🖫

FOR CATARRH, HAY FEVER, HEAD COLDS, ETC, PRICE, 50¢

VASES/PROFILES ILLUSION

What can you see? Is it a Holy Grail-like cup or two people about to kiss?

THE ALABAMA SYPHILIS EXPERIMENT

In 1997, President Bill Clinton made a formal apology on behalf of the United States to a small group of African-American survivors of a scandalous medical experiment. In 1932, more than 600 men from Tuskegee, Alabama, signed up for a government "medical study" that promised free healthcare and other benefits normally beyond the reach of the poorest U.S. citizens. Four hundred of the men suffered from syphilis, and it was to examine how this condition progressed when untreated that the experiment had actually been set up. Throughout the course of the study, the men with syphilis received no treatment, even though with the advent of penicillin it was available and improving in efficacy. The men themselves were led to believe that they were suffering from a disease known only as "bad blood." The deception ended in 1972, when it was exposed by the Associated Press agency. By this time, it was estimated that up to 100 of the men had died prematurely from their syphilis or related complications. Spouses, lovers, and children had been infected. Financial compensation was negotiated in the 1970s, but an apology took longer to arrive. ✍

ANIMAL LIES OR TRUTH #2

Lie: Dolphins can talk to each other underwater.
Truth: What they do is tune into each other's echolocation (the series of clicks they send out to reflect back off nearby obstacles or bodies) to remain aware of where each one is.

Lie: Elephants never forget.
Truth: They haven't even got the best memories in the animal kingdom—that goes to the turtles who will return to the exact same spot at which they were hatched to lay their eggs. This will usually be about 30 years later and may involve traveling distances of up to 2,400 miles. 💾

LIES ABOUT LIARS

Most people believe they can tell when someone's lying by the nervous way they behave—looking away and fidgeting, for example. Many law enforcement officers are trained to look out for inconsistent behavior and nervous body language as an indicator that someone is lying. But a wealth of psychological studies now show that liars rarely behave in this stereotypical way. Liars do not:

- Avoid eye contact and avert their gaze
- Act nervously and defensively
- Fidget and twitch
- Make unnecessary arm and hand gestures
- Clear their throats and pause frequently
- Stutter, umm, and er
- Look up to left or right while talking
- Bite their lips 📖

ROCK MYTHS EXPLODED #2

CHUBBY CHECKER INVENTED THE TWIST.

His hit single was a cover version of a tune written by Hank Ballard about a year before, when he composed the song to go with the twisting dance routines his backing band, The Midnighters, used to perform.

MICHAEL JACKSON BOUGHT THE BONES OF DAVID MERRICK, THE SO-CALLED ELEPHANT MAN, FROM A MUSEUM IN LONDON.

According to the museum, there were never even any enquiries made from the Jackson camp when the bones were put up for sale in the wake of the successful movie *The Elephant Man*. Neither did Michael Jackson appear anywhere in the movie.

MICHAEL JACKSON INVENTED THE MOONWALK.

No he didn't. It had been part of any competent street dancer's repertoire since the mid-1970s—Jacko didn't show it off with "Billie Jean" until 1983—and Shalamar's Jeffrey Daniel was performing it as part of their stage show in 1978.

CHRISSIE HYNDE (OF THE PRETENDERS) FIREBOMBED MCDONALD'S.

Ms. Hynde has been a vocal supporter of animal rights since coming to fame in the late 1970s. When, following a firebombing of one of their "restaurants" in Milton Keynes in England, the golden-arched giant threatened to take her to court for saying she did, she admitted what she said was a joke. 🖬

LIES WE TELL OURSELVES #3

As much as we may tell untruths to the government, our parents, partners, or children, we may also tell ourselves lies. Because we have to, and because it makes us feel better about ourselves.

"This shrank in the wash."—This is an out-and-out lie and we all know it. Virtually nothing shrinks in the wash in these days of the hyper-sensitive, artificially-intelligent washing machine. The simple fact is you've gained weight, you pig. This is the only explanation for too-tight clothing. (We're not talking hot-water washing jeans to make them fit snug as a girdle.) If something seems tight to you, don't assume you're not to blame. Gaining weight is, for most of us, too alarmingly easy to do and fretfully awful to undo. No wonder we lie to ourselves and say the clothes shrunk. The more weight we gain, the more we know we are slowing down. The next step? Death.

※ ※ ※

"We just need some time apart."— Some time? How about a few years or perhaps the rest of your life? Needing some time apart is how people let their romantic partners down easily. This is a lie, of course. You don't really need time apart. You need a new life, a new place to live and a new partner, preferably one who doesn't make you want to scream and gnash your teeth. Anyone who says that their partner has told them, "Oh, we just need some time

apart, but that's all," is seriously deluding themselves. They've been dumped. They don't know it yet.

※ ※ ※

"I work hard and I play hard."—This is how reprehensible misogynists/misandrists justify abusing those who love them and the dirty dealing they do which will, eventually, turn on them like a rabid dog. The thinking behind this is that if you work hard, then you are somehow given the right to be an ass. The lie of "I work hard and I play hard" is that they don't do either. They hate their work, treat people badly, and are hated by their employees or co-workers. To balance that, they find they must "play hard," which is to say get into fights, play games badly, cheat to win, and be a bad loser. Working hard and playing hard shouldn't be anything to brag about. They are actions, not banner statements to be admired and emulated.

※ ※ ※

"I work best under pressure."—A total lie that really means "I can't work to deadline nor can I plan ahead." People who say they work best under pressure cannot admit to themselves that they

are lazy, unmotivated individuals who wouldn't get much done if they weren't forced to do so. Working best under pressure is the lie we tell ourselves to cover up the fact that we aren't very disciplined in our endeavors; if mommy and daddy had left us a trust fund, we wouldn't even think we were best under pressure because, frankly, there wouldn't be any. Those with a lack of focus, lack of drive and ambition use this lie to comfort themselves. This is the only way they can compare to those who work ahead, get the job done well and early, and have a more balanced life because of it.

※　※　※

"I'm a people person."—This is the lie we tell ourselves when we realize that we spend most of our time talking and not accomplishing very much. "People" people don't really like to work very hard. They'd rather gossip about what is going on in the company or about a TV show the night before. If you are a motor mouth, you can add value to your overwhelming social skills (which dwarf all your other skills most likely) by saying that people are your best subject. If you are a maitre d' or work as a clerk, these are valuable skills to have, but only being able to chat to people, to stick your nose in their business and to give them your advice when they didn't ask for it is another matter. Don't think you're a people person when really all you are is a nosy person living vicariously through the acts of others. ❀

DIAMONDS FROM COAL

In 1905 Sir Julius Wernher, a governor of the famous De Beers Diamond Mines, was contacted by a Monsieur Henri Lemoine, who claimed he had invented a method of producing diamonds from coal. Would Sir Julius be interested in investing in the project?

Scientists at De Beers believed it was only a matter of time before a method of manufacturing diamonds would be discovered. Therefore, anxious to be in at the beginning of any form of mass production, which could easily destabilize the whole industry, Sir Julius visited Lemoine in his laboratory, accompanied by several associates also from De Beers.

Lemoine showed his guests into his laboratory, which had been set up with a furnace in the center and left the room. Minutes later, in the manner of a glamorous magician's assistant being miraculously produced from her cabinet, he re-entered the room in all his naked glory. Lemoine wished to prove that he was not concealing any diamonds about his person.

Lemoine placed some coal and several unidentified substances in a crucible and put the crucible in the furnace. Fifteen minutes later, he removed the crucible and, having allowed it to cool, sorted through the smoking contents with a pair of tweezers. One by one, around 20 small diamonds in total were produced.

Thinking that the diamonds suspiciously resembled those brought out of their own South African mines rather too closely, one of Sir Julius's De Beers associates demanded that Lemoine repeat the experiment. He did so promptly, this time producing 30 diamonds.

Despite having some reservations, it was vital that De Beers be in a position to be able to control or suppress this invention. Sir Julius therefore agreed to advance Lemoine the money for further research, on condition that it be kept a secret and providing he had first option on the formula, which would be kept sealed in a London bank. Lemoine readily agreed, of course.

Over the course of the next few years Sir Julius paid Lemoine a total of £64,000. However, in 1908 a Parisian jeweller admitted that he had sold Lemoine diamonds that were similar to, if not the same as, the ones produced in the experiment. Lemoine was brought to trial and given the chance to produce some more diamonds in front of the court. He failed and was indicted for fraud. He protested his innocence, but when the formula was unsealed it was found to be a simple mixture of carbon and sugar.

The fleet-footed Lemoine made a run for it and left the country before sentence could be passed. ✎

NEW ANTI-LIE TECHNOLOGY

Telling lies actually uses a different part of the brain from telling the truth. When subjects are tested with an EEG or electroencephalograph, an instrument for measuring brain wave patterns, in 9 out of 10 cases there is a "peak" in the trace when telling a lie. Other researchers have noticed a slight increase in blood flow around the eyes, which can be identified by a thermal-imaging camera. But the most exciting new lie-detecting development is called "brain fingerprinting," which uses brain scans to search for "guilty knowledge." When a murderer kills someone, they have intimate personal knowledge of the crime scene, as no innocent person does. Researchers have found that a specific brainwave named P300 responds automatically when it recognizes a familiar scene or object. In brain fingerprinting, suspects are shown a number of unfamiliar objects and those from the crime scene—a positive P300 response can suggest they have guilty knowledge of the crime. 📖

THE DONATION OF CONSTANTINE

This document, known in Latin as the *Donatio Constantini*, was one of the greatest forgeries of the Dark Ages. Dated A.D. 324, it purported to be an account of the conversion to Christianity of Constantine the Great, the first Roman emperor to adopt the new faith. As a measure of his gratitude, both for his religious awakening and the curing of his leprosy, he supposedly transferred temporal power over Rome, Italy, and the Western Empire to Pope Sylvester I and his suc-cessors. The Donation was included in a 9th-century collection of documents that became known as the False Decretals, as they contained a number of forgeries that supported the power of the papacy. From the 11th century onwards, the Donation was increasingly cited by popes to assert their authority in temporal matters. But in 1440, the Italian humanist Lorenzo Valla showed that the document was an 8th-century fake, composed in either Rome or the Frankish Empire. ✍

LIES WE TELL TEENAGERS

"IF YOU DON'T COME HOME, I'LL TEAR UP YOUR DRIVER'S LICENSE!"

By morning, they'll be too tired to tear up your license, and anyway, it is laminated so this threat is meaningless.

"GOOD GIRLS DON'T SMOKE IN THE STREET."

Well, maybe not. But a lot of regular girls do and I guess I am one of those.

"IT IS POLITE TO WRITE THANK YOU NOTES FOR GIFTS AND PARTIES."

Yes, it is polite. Alas, society as it currently stands is *not* polite. In fact, you look bad if you do send a note. It looks as if you have nothing else to do, no friends, and that you rarely get gifts or invitations to places. So, call and say thank you if you must but otherwise, don't bother.

"GOOD GIRLS DON'T WEAR EYELINER ON THEIR LOWER LIDS."

Yeah, if you want to look like a freshly washed, super-clean inhabitant of a religious order you shouldn't wear eyeliner on your lower lids.

"FILL UP THE CAR WITH GAS AND CHECK THE OIL IF YOU ARE GOING TO USE IT."

Why should I when you will? Taking care of the car is one of those things you do only when you're already in trouble or you want something more than using the car that evening or for the weekend. You may want to sell the car for cash, for example, or take it to South America. These are good reasons for checking the oil and keeping it filled.

"IF BILL POTTER JUMPED OFF THE EMPIRE STATE BUILDING, YOU WOULD TOO."

Well, maybe I would. Frankly, imitating my peer group and doing stuff other people of my age group do is really important to me. If I wanted to stand out in a crowd, don't you think I'd do it my own way? It is vital to keep in with the in crowd if you are already in the in crowd.

"WAIT TILL YOU HAVE KIDS. THEN YOU'LL KNOW."

Yes, I will know, if I have kids, what you are going through now. Or more precisely what I am putting you through. But that will be some years off and I won't be as anal (or, perhaps, as good a parent) as you are now. Some of us forgot to have children and so we'll never know what it is like.

"SO, YOU FORGOT TO GET GROCERIES BUT YOU REMEMBERED TO PLAY YOUR GAME? I'LL PRETEND TO FORGET TO MAKE DINNER."

It isn't as if we are scraping the bottom here for food. Most of us are overweight and so missing a meal or 40 would actually be a good thing. Oh, and I got a really high score on my game so that's good.

"YOU BROKE THIS [X]."

Now that's a harsh accusation. Better to ask, "Did I break it on purpose?" or "How did this get broken?" I am not about to admit to breaking something when it is clear you are already on the rampage about it. I can only lie.

"WHY CAN'T YOU BE LIKE YOUR [X]? HE/SHE'S SO [POSITIVE PREDICATE]."

If they're good, why didn't you just give me away? I am different than they are and I make mistakes and, I guess, we all have our own gifts. It seems I haven't found mine yet and you like *theirs* better anyway. If you're going to have children, don't play obvious favorites. Later you'll have to lie and say . . .

"I LOVE YOU ALL EQUALLY BUT DIFFERENTLY."

This is a complete lie. You love the one you love better than the ones you don't love as much. Fathers love their daughters more; mothers side with their sons. Some kids everyone hates because they are just, well, weird. You can't like them all, even though, as parents, that is your job.

"IF YOU'RE GOOD, I'LL GET YOU A PONY."

Careful if you say this. Of course, it may not be a pony. Maybe it is a cell phone, skateboard, or Porsche. But children remember comments like this and, as the Chinese proverb says, "A lie is worse than a broken bone." If you don't get us that pony, we'll either go through life with a broken heart, save up for the darned thing, or not trust you the rest of your life.

"THIS WILL HURT A LITTLE," OR, "THIS WON'T HURT AT ALL."

This means that it will hurt like the bejesus. Better to say, jokingly, "This will hurt me more than it will hurt you" or, better yet, say nothing before the pain and afterwards, look at your child with a wicked face and smile, "Did that hurt?" Look as if you are getting immense satisfaction out of their pain. This will either make them a bit mentally unbalanced or imbue them with a sense of humor.

"I'D LOVE YOU MORE IF YOU WERE GOOD."

No parent should ever say this. If they do and it isn't a lie, it should be. ❀

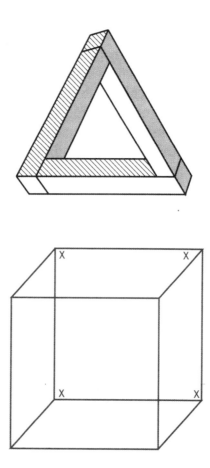

Top: the Penrose impossible triangle. Following the similarly shaded sides gets you nowhere.
Bottom: Where are the crosses? On the back side of the cube or on the top side looking down?

WHO ARE YOU CALLING AN AMERICAN LIAR?

The White Pages telephone directory online service (whitepages.com) lists only three Liars in the whole of the United States. They are Beverley Liar (a doctor) in Enterprise, Alabama; Kim Liar of Houston, Texas; and Vicki McCloud Liar who lives in Charleston, West Virginia. There are no listings at all for anyone named A. Liar. 📖

THE POLICE KNOW WHEN YOU'RE LYING

Figures of authority have always been afforded supernatural powers of deduction and knowlege. In ancient times a god would be invoked in order to extract a confession from a "criminal"—the accused would be told that the gods had seen what they had done and punish them accordingly.

In more recent times the science of criminal deduction has developed ever more sophisticated methods to determine the guilt or otherwise of an accused suspect. However, the process of determining criminal guilt begins at a police station where, one would hope, officers can easily deduce guilt.

Aldert Vrij and Samantha Mann, both psychologists at the University of Portsmouth in England, published a study in the March–April 2001 edition of *Applied Cognitive Psychology* magazine which assessed, for the first time, people's ability to size up a highly motivated liar. For their study, Vrij and Mann obtained a video tape of two police officers interviewing a murder suspect. Although the suspect denied knowing and killing the victim,

evidence later showed that he was lying. The suspect then confessed in a second videotaped police interview and was convicted of murder.

The researchers selected six segments from the interviews. Three showed the suspect lying about his activities on the day of the murder. The remaining segments featured truthful statements.

Of 65 police officers shown the segments, 18 made no more than one error in detecting lies and truths. Another 36 judged 3 or 4 segments correctly, and the remaining 11 identified only 1 or 2 segments correctly. Because the words were unrecognizable, they had to detect lies using non-verbal cues and speech intonations.

This translates to the police being able to recognize a liar in their custody at least 65% of the time. Further research carried out by Vrij with police officers in lab studies found that they were usually correct in spotting lies 70% of the time. Previous laboratory-based research into detecting liars resulted in a 55% success rate for non-police officers. 📖

SELLING LIES #2

Ever since man decided that the best way to live was in a capitalist society where everything has its price and everything can be bought and sold, men have excelled in the art of selling. In this, our age of the eternal selling, men can now sell to us "virtually" and with such subtlety that we can often not notice that we've purchased something until the bill for it arrives. Here are some more of the seller's greatest lies. If you hear or read these words, beware.

"APPLY FOR A LOW FIXED-RATE CARD"

Trouble is, there is no such thing. Fixed means "whatever rate they want" really. Credit card companies can also change the rate whenever they wish. So, you may sign up for a 1.2% APR but end up with 23%. All they have to do is send you written notice. There's another catch too: pay late and you get to pay even more with an added on penalty rate. There is also a wonderful little clause called a universal default policy, where if you pay other bills late you automatically default on your credit card and get a penalty tacked onto that too. Remember: cash is cash. And cash is king.

"FREE PHONE CALLS"

Even free phone calls over the internet aren't, at the minute, genuinely free. Some companies may offer 1 cent per minute calls to Guam, but they will charge you whatever they want to put in that sneaky small print for extra added "connection charges" or line rental or use of the air around your phone. Advertised rates often mean little or nothing once all of the ifs, ands, and buts are built into the "free" scheme that sounds so promising. There is no such thing as a free lunch; in fact, beware of that little word called "free." It is one of the biggest lies ever told.

"FREE TRAVEL FOR 25,000 MILES"

There's that little "free" word again, which should be setting bells off in your head or in your wallet. Frequent flier programs are a little easier than they used to be but they are still rife with problems. For starters, the rules are byzantine in complexity: for one large international airline, you can only get miles if you fly in C or H class. Trouble is, no one can tell you whether you *are* flying C or H class and so you cannot know, until you fill in your online form, if the flight you've booked actually accrues any air-mile mileage. Another problem is redemption. Trying to use miles you have will show you how meaningless the word "free" can really be. Airlines cunningly don't let on that you are competing with a billion other travelers to get frequent flier seats. Strangely enough, a lot of people want to go where it is hot during the winter. So unless you actually want to fly to Minnesota in the dead of January, frequent flier miles are a nest of trouble. Ultimately, you're paying for the flight anyway with your assured loyalty to the airline. Commonly, if you check the best available prices, you can usually get a better-priced, better-scheduled flight without using your miles at all. How's that for "free?"

"YOU NEED TO HAVE YOUR RECEIPT"

Uh, no, you don't in many cases, if you can prove that you bought it in other ways. Many computer outlet stores will have records of purchases which will act as a receipt. Often, keeping the original bag with the original tag will be enough evidence of the sale, particularly if they have electronic inventory codes. So even if they say no return without a ticket, they could be lying. There is always another way of returning something—even if it means you have to buy something else.

"IT WILL FIT BETTER WITH WEAR"

Unless something is made out of leather (which gives) or denim (which sometimes gives), if an item of clothing doesn't fit you now, it never will. This includes jackets that are too long, pants that are too short, and skirts that are too tight. Losing weight to get into a different size rarely works. So don't believe the salesperson when they tell you this lie or, perhaps the best one of all, "That looks great on you" when, with it being bright green with a flouncy sleeve, you know it doesn't. In fact, it would look bad on anyone, living or dead. Of course, if you are shopping for a bridesmaid dress, nothing will look good on you because that's the traditional bride's evil plan. The clue to buying great clothing? If it makes you feel as if you want to wear it out of the shop, buy it. ❁

"YOU'LL NEVER MISS THE WATER"

DEVIL'S FORK ILLUSION

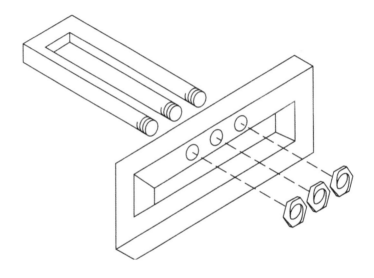

A three-pronged fork slotting precisely into a uniform hollowed-out rectangular box, right?
Wrong. Look more closely and you'll see that neither of these objects is physically possible.

ENDANGERED SPECIES

There are so many endangered animal species in Florida that it is going to be
fenced off and all its residents relocated to Alabama. 🖫◗

A GOPHER WILL FETCH YOU THINGS

But they'll eat them on the way back. 🖫◗

THE FEEJEE MERMAID

In 1842 the well-known impresario and
showman P. T. Barnum added an exhibit
known as the Feejee Mermaid to the
collection housed in his museum of
curiosities. A Dr. J. Griffin, an English
naturalist, was said to have discovered
the mermaid near the island of Feejee,
hence its name. Barnum advertised his
new exhibit in the press accompanied
by an illustration of a comely young
mermaid, of exactly the kind that the
word "mermaid" generally conjures up.
Unfortunately, in reality the Feejee
Mermaid was very far removed from the
beautiful creature that the public had
been led to expect. In the first place it
was dead, and in the second it was
exceedingly ugly, a long way from the
long-maned curvaceous creatures that
lure sailors to their death with their
haunting song and alluring beauty. It
had a monkey-like head and upper
body with a withered, scaly tail. The
whole thing was distinctly unappeal-
ing, if not downright repellent.

Barnum had bought the mermaid
second-hand and had decided to whet
the public's appetite in the press of the
day with a little Victorian hyperbole.
Dr. Griffin was in fact an associate of
Barnum called Levi Lynum, whom
Barnum hired to pose as its discoverer.
The so-called "mermaid" itself was a
composite creature fashioned out of a
monkey's head and torso, which was
attached to the tail of a salmon. ✑

BOOK BLURB LIES #2

"An inimitable style"

This is an out-and-out publishing lie. This means, in fact, that the author has a very easily and often imitated style. It's the sort of thing you'd say about Stephen King, Graham Greene, or Herman Melville. Not about, well, those other writers who are merely derivative.

"Breakneck speed"

But we don't want to break our necks on a story, do we? Any book written or said to be written in this style brings up the question of why we are rushing to read this book. Is it, itself, written as such in an attempt to get itself over and done with? Or did the author make the mistake of ordering a double shot of espresso when she actually wanted the decaf latte? NB: Not to be confused with "a cracking pace," which is about the right speed.

"Darkly comic"

This means it isn't quite funny enough to be funny on its own. It has to rely on being sarcastic and cruel about people and events. This sort of thing you do at home.

"Deceptively simple"

It's simple. Whoever wrote the report or the review must have been watching television while reading. Nothing is deceptive about a simple book, unless it is sold in the jaws of an unsprung mantrap.

"Deftly written"

The author got the manuscript into us on time. Although to say someone writes deftly is to commend them, the word is bandied about so much that it has almost lost its meaning. Deft (meaning "dexterous") could apply to the author's ability to hold a pen or, moreover, how quickly they can type. Expect sentences. Lots of them.

"Destined to make it big"

The author is my friend or I have bought the film rights to the story. So please buy the darned book and make this sentence true. (Check that the author isn't either related to the publisher or is a girlfriend/boyfriend thereof.)

"Edgy"
Parts of this book need a good wash. Or the person really likes Brett Easton Ellis but can't quite swing it.

"Emotional roller coaster"
What, with ups and downs and candy and throwing up and needing to be *this* tall to ride it and everything? I think not. It is emotional. Maybe melodramatic. Certainly it is about feeling stuff—and not with your hands either.

"Epic"
Too long.

"Exhaustive"
The author ignored his family so much that he was divorced by the books' publication date. Or, like Mary Lou in 8th grade with her report on New Mexico, he just didn't know when to stop. No one likes these kinds of people except those who like a good-looking yet unopened book for their vast snobby home library.

"Having an appeal for both serious scholar and layman reader"
There are lots of pictures, to heck with the serious scholar part. This book, although clothed as an erudite volume, is just this short of being a comic book. It is fun but doesn't want you to know that.

"Hits the ground running"
This story has been edited to smithereens. Readers should count themselves lucky though because the boring first few chapters have been skillfully excised. So the story begins here, i.e., in a good place to make you want to read the thing.

"Has a keen eye"
Usually used to "sharply observe" or to produce "sharp observations." This doesn't mean the writer actually possesses good eyesight. Most authors do not. In fact, most authors wear glasses or contacts in order to see what they're writing. When they make it big, they will get their eyes lasered. Then and only then can they genuinely be said to have "a keen eye." ❁

THE TOP 10 LIES WE TELL OUR CHILDREN

1. We found you under a bush.
2. If the wind changes you'll stay like that.
3. If you're not asleep, Santa won't come.
4. It's all gone.
5. The shop was closed.
6. Fluffy's going to sleep for a long time.
7. What a beautiful painting.
8. You're so good at that.
9. We're nearly there.
10. This won't hurt.

SUPERSTAR LIES

Tom Cruise is only 4 feet 3 inches tall, and the sets on all his films are specially constructed so he appears normal sized.

Pamela Anderson starts to melt if she stands too near a radiator for too long.

Colin Farrell has drawings of every pair of shoes he's ever owned.

Kate Winslet's nickname is The Yeti because she has size 14 feet.

That is Bruce Willis's very own vest and he's under contract not to throw it away, no matter how dirty, ripped, or sweaty it gets.

Ferris Bueller never had a day off in his life.

Sylvester Stallone "cried like a bitch" when he got hit during the fight scenes in *Rocky*.

Keanu Reeves was acting in *Bill & Ted's Excellent Adventure*.

As a teenager Halle Berry was meat-pie eating champion of Cleveland, Ohio.

William Shatner's "hair."

Pierce Brosnan's James Bond contract prevents him from wearing a dinner jacket in any other film.

9/11 LIES

The following is taken from **http://homepage.ntlworld.com/steve seymour/lies911/lies.htm** and it claims that the telephone call from TV pundit Barbara Olson to her husband Ted's office (he worked for the U.S. Justice Department) from onboard the American Airlines plane that ploughed into the Pentagon on 9/11 could not have taken place.

"She [Barbara] had trouble getting through, because she wasn't using her cell phone—she was using the phone in the passengers' seats," said Mr. Olson. "I guess she didn't have her purse, because she was calling collect, and she was trying to get through to the Department of Justice, which is never very easy." . . . "She wanted to know 'What can I tell the pilot? What can I do? How can I stop this?'" The forged Barbara Olson telephone call claims that the flight deck crew were with her at the back of the aircraft, presumably politely ushered down there by the box cutter-wielding Muslim maniacs, who for some bizarre reason decided not to cut their throats on the flight deck. Have you ever heard anything quite so ridiculous?

But it is at this juncture that we finally have the terminal error. Though the American Airlines Boeing 757 is fitted with individual telephones at each seat position, they are not of the variety where you can simply pick up the handset and ask for an operator. On many aircraft you can talk from one seat to another in the aircraft free of charge, but if you wish to access the outside world you must first swipe your credit card through the telephone. By Ted Olson's own admission, Barbara did not have a credit card with her.

It gets worse. On American Airlines there is a telephone set-up charge of $2.50, which can only be paid by credit card, then a $2.50 (sometimes $5.00) charge per minute of speech thereafter. The set-up charge is really the crucial element. Without paying it in advance by swiping your credit card you cannot access the external telephone network. Under these circumstances the passengers' seat phones on a Boeing 757 are of as much use as plastic toys. Perhaps Ted Olson made a mistake and Barbara managed to borrow a credit card from a fellow passenger? Not a chance. If Barbara had done so, once swiped through the phone, the credit card would have enabled her to call whoever she wanted to for as long as she liked, negating any requirement to call collect. Sadly perhaps, the Olson telephone call claim is proved untrue. Any American official wishing to challenge this has only to subpoena the telephone company and Justice Department records. There will be no charge originating from American Airlines 77 to the U.S. Solicitor General. 📖

FOOD LIES #2

Do you ever suspect that some food is named just to confuse you? Forget about the ridiculous lists of ingredients on labels, with their pseudo-scientific names and ridiculously long spellings. We all understand that they're named thus in order to not alarm us. What we're concerned with here are the articles you are faced with that have totally misleading names. Take the foodstuffs listed here. Their very names are lies:

※　※　※

Mincemeat—There's no meat in mincemeat these days, but in olden times, ground meat was added to a mixture of dried fruits and liquor to create a special treat around the holidays. Recently, a popular TV chef reconstructed the traditional mincemeat recipe using lamb or veal. As the meat flavor disappears into the sweetness of the dried fruits, it is easy to see why cost-conscious cooks would leave out the expensive meat in the dish yet keep its name—a name which suggests more luxurious fare.

※　※　※

Spotted Dick—A form of suet pudding (a heavy, starchy sweet) studded with dried fruits. There is no trace of anything that could remotely be called "dick" or "Richard" although in the mid 19th century, "dick" did suggest a hard cheese which, when served with a sugar sauce, was served as a dessert.

※　※　※

Submarine Sandwich—A sandwich made in a long bun or roll, which is then split along its length and filled with layered meat, cheese, tomatoes, lettuce, and various condiments. The "sub" is so called because it resembles a submarine but the sandwich is also called the Cuban, grinder, hero, hoagie, Italian, poor boy, torpedo, wedge, and zep (from zeppelin). The sandwich was never served onboard a submarine nor does it include parts of a submarine, decommissioned or otherwise.

※　※　※

S*** On A Shingle—Thank goodness there isn't any actual excrement of any sort in this recipe originating in World War I. Called "shit on a shingle," the mass-catering recipe was actually chipped beef on toast but called "s.o.s." because of its rather unappetizing appearance.

※　※　※

Porcupine Balls—Although many Americans have eaten exotic local meats such as possum and squirrel, porcupine remains a relatively unsavored animal. Porcupine balls are not made of this spikey animal but rather traditional meatballs made of hamburger or other minced meat spiked with cooked white rice. This gives the balls an appearance of having tiny quills within the meat itself.

※　※　※

Mom's Apple Pie—While there shouldn't be any trace of your mother in Mom's apple pie, there are doubts that anyone's mother actually makes any pie that bears the moniker of Mom's Apple Pie. Unless your mother is a food industrialist, you won't find a true example of Mom's Apple Pie served in any commercial establishment. Even worse, some pies that are so-called don't even have any apple in them, being made from cheese biscuits soaked in a vinegar and cinnamon solution with sugar.

※　※　※

Homemade anything—Foods that are homemade are rarely labeled so. Usually, a homemade foodstuff will look the part, being stowed in homely mason jars or topped with wax, string, paper, and other sealing ingredients that wouldn't stand the test of the supermarket much less the FDA. For something to be truly homemade, it must be made in someone's home—and usually that home isn't an enormous factory that also makes auto parts.

※　※　※

Baked Alaska—Has very little to do with Alaska. This frozen and baked confection was a popular show-off dish in America in the 1950s. A slab of ice cream is surrounded by stiffly whipped egg whites to form a sort of igloo effect. The whole creation is shoved into the oven to grill enough to color the outside of the egg whites but not melt the ice cream in the middle. A precursor to deep fried ice cream often found in Mexican eateries. ▦

HEINRICH SCHLIEMANN
AND KING PRIAM'S TREASURE

Heinrich Schliemann appointed himself "creator of Greek prehistoric archaeology." He was born in Germany in 1822 and died in 1890. The many biographies written about him tell of an extraordinary life—one informed by a small childhood experience. At the age of 7, he said in his autobiography, he saw an illustration of Troy in flames. The walls of the city looked so strong, thought the boy, that they must still be there.

Schliemann's childhood was difficult. He was one of 7, and when his mother died his father began a relationship with a maid. Heinrich argued with his father. He got TB. He had to work hard in a grocery store and then as a cabin boy. However, by most accounts, when he reached his early 20s, life began to turn around. While traveling to meet his brother in the States, he got to meet the President, Zachary Taylor, and his family.

There were more adventures to be had in the U.S. It was peak gold rush time, and Heinrich made his own pile of $350,000 by buying gold dust from miners in Sacramento. He also recorded being witness to the Great Fire in San Francisco in 1851. Next he visited Greece for the first time.

At 46, after more traveling and study in Paris, he began his career as an archaeologist. This he did in bold style.

In Mycenae, Greece, he put forward a theory that royal tombs would be found inside the city walls, as opposed to outside. He then obtained a doctorate—after writing his thesis in ancient Greek—and married a 16-year-old Greek girl, Sophie, with the blessing of her parents, who were impressed at his worldliness.

Schliemann's next project was to search for Troy, which he was convinced was a real place—and if Homer was to be believed, a place with gold. On the basis of his readings of Homer, he decided that the city was to be found nearer the sea than archaeologists had so far searched, at Hissarlik in Turkey.

Archeologically speaking there were rich pickings there. Clear evidence of settlement existed—in fact several cities on top of each other. Schliemann was interested only in "Troy," so his men were ordered to ignore the first settlements and investigate what lay beneath. After 12 years, say the biographers, Schliemann found his treasure, having seen a glint through a hole in a wall. Secretly he and Sophie collected it—gold jewelry and drinking vessels. Schliemann's discoveries were announced in Athens and he became world famous.

Then in 1972, 82 years after Schliemann had died at the age of 68,

William Calder, professor of classics at Colorado University, began making checks. He established that almost the only source for the information contained within the biographies was the subject himself. He then went to the University of Rostock, where he found the thesis, but only a tiny section of it was in ancient Greek and this was very badly written. Next to newspaper accounts of Schliemann meeting the president. There were none—he had

but although it is uncertain who found the majority of it, it was probably not Heinrich Schliemann. There are too many problems with his account. He did not mention the discovery of the treasure in his journals, a description of what he found in the first draft of a book he was writing does not describe any sort of treasure in existence—and his wife was not there at the time because she was in Athens mourning the death of her father.

made it up. Schliemann was unraveling.

David Trail, professor of classics at California University, made further checks. Schliemann had made money from gold dust sure enough, but it had involved cheating miners; he had not been in San Francisco on the date of the fire, and the account of it in his diary—which had the wrong date on it—had been glued in later; he had never even seen the burning Troy illustration as a child. Calder's view was that Schliemann was a pathological liar.

So what of the treasure that made his reputation? Such treasure exists,

The great irony and sadness about Heinrich Schliemann's lies is that his true archaeological pedigree, at least, would have been perfectly illustrious without them. Against the judgment of many eminent scholars of the time and preceding him, his hunches led to the discovery of ancient cities in Hissarlik and the royal tombs at Mycenae; these alone are career-making finds. Instead, because of his desire to rewrite his life story as something more thrilling and romantic, he will be remembered as a compulsive liar and a cheat who people were taken in by until decades after his death. ⚱

LIES WOMEN TELL MEN #2

"I think you have beautiful ears."—The lie that means, "You are ugly but I really want you to marry me so I'll overlook that part." Some women are willing to do anything for love and attention. Of course, this is not restricted to women: men often say the thing they like about the women they date is the fact they have a pulse. Women, however, look past a man's fatal flaws—the lack of a brain, no teeth, etc.—and will tell you so. They will actually tell you that they love certain parts of you, cautiously omitting the other larger, unlovable areas. They are lying of course.

❈ ❈ ❈

"You know, I never notice how tall men are/how much hair men have."—The lie that means, "I am pretty desperate for a boyfriend right now." There comes a time in some women's lives when they realize that if beauty is skin deep, ugly goes straight to the bone. They also realize that if they were thinking about having good-looking children, they should have made that their life goal rather than waiting this long and seeing that all the good ones are taken. Good looks are important for women but, when they get to the two-cats-and-a-bottle-of-vodka stage of life, they're more than willing to lie to you and tell you that they don't notice your large hairy mole, nor your third eye or nipple.

❈ ❈ ❈

"I don't expect you to pay for everything."—The lie that means, "You should pay for everything if you think I'm going to like you at all." Women try to be fair but this entails lying. Every woman feels that she should be treated by a man, no matter how liberated or wealthy she may be. She will have to tell a fib, though, to get you to see that she is a modern woman—up to a point. Offer to pay anyway. Or, if you don't like her, tell her you expect her to pay. Liars should not prosper too much, should they?

❋ ❋ ❋

"I love football/live bands/drinking myself to death."—The lie that means, "I will get you for my boyfriend if it means I have to have a sex change." This lifestyle lie will become apparent if you accidentally marry a woman who, mysteriously, seems to adapt to your very existence during the months or years of courtship. If you've found a woman who loves the same club, the same band, and the same booze you do, be certain she is lying. She will inevitably snap back into her true character after she has what she wants. Or when she's tired.

❋ ❋ ❋

"Shopping? I never shop!"—The lie that means, "You know all those girl things you hate? I am hiding all that behavior so you'll like me." Men hate shopping. Women know this. So they will lie to make themselves seem special and exotic and valuable to you. A woman who doesn't shop means she won't ask you for money, decorating, clothing, or child advice. She'll be a woman who is self-initiating. She can make her own decisions. Sooner or later, however, unless you like living in a hovel, someone is going to have to go shopping. Strangely enough, the she-liar will offer her services.

❋ ❋ ❋

"Your friends are so sweet!"—The lie that means, "Your friends are dumber than a box of hair at the barbershop." The word "sweet" is an outright lie. No one is sweet. They're either dumb or silly or wacky or odd. If a woman says your friends are darlings, adorable, marvelous, or any of those other words, be assured she is lying. She only wants you to think she likes them so you will like her more. Most of all, look out for the word "nice." This will be said, in future reference to your friends, between her clenched teeth.

❋ ❋ ❋

"That guy? I hardly know him."—The lie that means, "I married him, had his children, defended him in court and I am still seeing him behind your back but otherwise . . . no. Hardly know the guy." Again, the lady doth protest (i.e., lie) too much. Don't expect any women to be virginal, ever. Do you care where she's honed her man-handling skills? Do you care that she may still be spending time with Mr. Hairy Knuckles? Lie and say no. ✿

NOT WHO THEY SAY THEY ARE #2

For some reason many famous actors have chosen to drop the name that their parents thought long and hard before giving them, and replace it with something that they (or their studio) feel is far more "fitting." With some actors the decision was undoubtedly a good one—see Goldie Hawn—while for others you have to ask, why bother?

IS NOW	WAS ONCE
Alan Alda	Alphonso D'Abruzzo
Woody Allen	Allen Konigsberg
Julie Andrews	Julia Wells
Charles Bronson	Charles Buchinski
Mel Brooks	Melvin Kaminsky
Ellen Burstyn	Edna Gilhooley
Michael Caine	Maurice Micklewhite
Sean Connery	Tom Connery
Tom Cruise	Thomas Mapother IV
Kirk Douglas	Issur Danielovitch
Blake Edwards	William McEdwards
Whoopi Goldberg	Caryn Johnson
Cary Grant	Archie Leach
Goldie Hawn	Jean Studlendgehawn
Rita Hayworth	Margarita Cansino

IS NOW	WAS ONCE
Michael Keaton	Michael Douglas
Jude Law	Dave Law
Marilyn Monroe	Norma Jean Mortenson
Demi Moore	Demi Guynes
Brad Pitt	William Pitt
Winona Ryder	Winona Horowitz
Tupac Shakur	Tetrapak One Shaker
Martin Sheen	Ramon Estevez
Christian Slater	Christian Hawkins
Biggie Smalls	Shortass Biggs
Christopher Walken	Ronnie Walken
John Wayne	Marion Morrison
Sigourney Weaver	Susan Weaver
Gene Wilder	Jerry Silberman

WHY PATHOLOGICAL LIARS LIE

Although there might be some genetic component to lying—studies on twins raised apart suggest some congenital similarities in their tendency to lie—other brain dysfunctions are more likely to encourage pathological lying. People with borderline or narcissistic personality disorders who function in an impulsive and chaotic way often become chronic liars. Through the thrill of successfully passing off a lie, a narcissistic person gains power and energy and feels superior to the person they've taken in, which psychologists suggest may be the underlying motivation that drives con-men, fraudsters, and, perhaps to a lesser extent, even salesmen.

Those with borderline personality disorders often spread destructive rumors and lies about the people around them—for example, they claim that their partner beats them or is a sexual abuser—in order to devalue that person and vent their own anger on them.

Children who grow up with alcoholic or drug-addicted parents also tend to become proficient liars, perhaps to protect themselves from upset and violence or to conceal and deny to themselves and the world what's really happening in their family lives. Other chronic liars—who perhaps picked up the habit to protect themselves from intrusive parents—lie to keep people at a distance. By creating a tissue of lies and distortions about their lives, habits, and feelings, they protect and nurture their own autonomous sense of self from invasion by others. 📖

HOLLYWOOD DREAMS

DON'T BELIEVE EVERYTHING THAT YOU SEE IN THE MOVIES, OR HEAR IN LOS ANGELES.

Paul Newman really ate all those eggs in *Cool Hand Luke*.

A group of Hollywood film executives invented feng shui at a dinner party in Laurel Canyon in 1984.

Dustin Hoffman wants to play a Yorkshire terrier, but can't get the accent right.

Winona Ryder was "going to pay for it."

Hugh Grant was "researching a part."

It is Julia Roberts on the posters for *Pretty Woman*.

Scene-restoring "director's cuts" actually improve anything. 💾

OFF WITH HER HEAD

Just because she was a lowly and not very well paid bank clerk, Parisian Francoise H. didn't see why she should not enjoy as many rare and expensive 17th-century antiques as her bank could afford. So she bought some gilt mirrors, ornate wooden panels, a wardrobe, a Regency chest of drawers, and a Louis XIV commode along with a bunch of cherubins. She added a huge, canopied bed that was unfortunately too big for her three-room apartment in the middle-class Parisian suburb of Montreuil, so she kept it in pieces in her entrance hall, and charged the lot to her bank, covering her tracks by listing the purchases as stationery.

Despite the final bill for the antiques coming to around $18 million, it took Ms. H.'s bosses from 2002 until 2005 to realize that despite pay-ing such a huge invoice for pens, they were still running out of ballpoints by Friday afternoon. When she was finally investigated it was discovered that Ms. H. had spent almost $9 million at the 2004 Paris Biennale Antiques Fair and that she was—unsurprisingly—a regular at the many grand private sales among the best Parisian antiques fairs. None of the antiques dealers thought that it was odd that a woman such as Ms. H. should live in a small apartment and yet spend huge amounts of money, apparently. She told them that she had inherited the money and was staying in Montreuil temporarily until she found a palace for sale. On being confronted with accusations of her crimes, Ms. H. admitted having lied to her bosses. She did not admit lying to antiques dealers, though . . . 📖

JESUS ILLUSION

Stare at the few dots in the center of the image for 20 to 30 seconds, then look away and stare at a blank white wall. What do you see?

ADVERTISING LIES #2

"AND THERE'S SO MUCH MORE!"
Actually, there isn't any "more" but we paid for the space and we're going to use it. Any place that claims to have more than they can mention in an advertisement usually sells nothing but run-offs, end of lines, samples, and some stuff that their cousin brought over from his store.

"SAVINGS OF UP TO 80%!"
Any reduction of price will be on nothing that fits you, that matches anything in your home, that you could use as a gift, or that you would want anywhere near your person. Items that are so marked down are usually low-priced for a reason. In this case, the one item that may make that offer of 80% reduction possibly true would only fit one person and he lives in Guam.

"THE CUSTOMER ALWAYS COMES FIRST."
The customer does not always come first. This is obvious to anyone who has waited while a clerk or service person either chats to their friend behind the counter or spends 10 minutes making a personal call on their cell. The customer is the enemy. The customer is the person who makes the clerk's day

a living hell so why would they want to treat them well? The statement that the customer is always right is only something sellers tell buyers to placate them. The customer does not always come first but they often come at the wrong moment. This kind of treatment usually goes hand in hand with stores that advertise themselves as putting "people first."

"HAVE A NICE DAY."

If only they said it like they meant it. If only the sentence had any meaning coming from a stranger. But when an employee who is obviously longing to go on a break wearily lies to you, snap back, "Don't tell me what to do" as a suitable reply.

"THANK YOU FOR SHOPPING AT . . ."

Another total lie, the clerk doesn't care whether you shopped at their particular store or not. Although the owners might, making their employees utter in parrot-like repetition these meaning-free sounds, transforming the workers into nothing more than walking sandwich boards. This is not a genuine thank you.

"YOUR OPINION MATTERS TO US."

A seller's lie. The consumer's opinion rarely matters. As long as enough people keep buying stuff, the store owners will be extremely happy to keep things as they are. If, say, 10% of the customers complain, business carries on as usual. Any consumer who believes that their opinion really does matter to the store management should realize that they are not important customers, they are seen as mere sheep with wallets, waiting to be shorn. This extends to similar phrases such as, "You are a valued customer," and "Your time is important to us."

"THIS IS A REAL SURVEY."

No, it isn't, as you will find out if you stop for the survey takers on the street. After 15 minutes of yapping about a social issue (athlete's foot, the state of women's shoe design, etc.), the survey taker will suddenly ask, "So, what bank do you use?" or "What airline do you frequent the most?" If you ask at this point whether the survey is real or not, the taker will most likely say, "Er, no."

"WE CARE ABOUT YOU."

Trying to get good service where the individual employees couldn't care less isn't a matter of company policy. It is a matter of personal policy. That is why when a company brays about "caring," it should impress no one. For all the training they give their staff, the only reasons we shop at a particular place are because 1 or 2 of the ground staff actually do their job, it is close to home, or incredibly affordable. ✿

LIES COUPLES TELL #2

As with the Lies Women Tell Men, the course of human relationships and particularly those involving love, rarely run true. The following are examples of some of the lies that men and women tell each other when they're in love.

❋ ❋ ❋

"I never think about anyone else during sex."—Liar liar, pants on fire! Whether it is the young Mel Gibson or Colin Farrell or Will Ferrell or Lassie, every normal person takes a star to bed with them once in a while in their minds. Sometimes, you may have intimate relations with an ex, or someone you just met; the only difference is that you are using your partner's body to make the whole event a little more interactive. In many ways, making love with your partner while thinking about someone else—maybe even yourself—is the most primitive form of virtual sex. You can't tell them that, though. You have to lie. Otherwise they'll never forgive you and you will hurt their itty bitty feelings.

❋ ❋ ❋

"No, that's fine."—Doesn't matter what it is, it isn't fine. It is never fine. This is a lie that occurs when partners realize that arguing sometimes gets less than nothing done. This lie is used while ordering from a menu, at the end of a long discussion where no useful conclusion is reached, or when you are too tired to talk anymore. Be assured that when your partner says, "No, that's fine," they are lying through their teeth. Nothing could be further than fine. Want to know what fine really is? Fine is when you capitulate, agree with what they are saying, do it wholeheartedly and fully with a large genuine smile on your face. It will never be fine as long as you are you and they are them.

❋ ❋ ❋

"I love it when you tell that story."—Another lie. This one is often told with a slight edge to it in the early days of the relationship, before both of you know the sound of nastiness in the other's voice. Relationships are like wheels: they go around. Some days you may actually not be lying when your partner is telling that dumb story that they always tell—you may like it because you are trying to make a play for the person sitting next to you. As long as your windbag partner is yapping, you're free. Then again, you may grow immune to the story's pain or laughter and feel quite neutral about it. And long after your partner leaves you, you'll think of that story fondly. But right now, you lie and say you love it.

"I'd love to have your friends over."—This lie operates in the tit-for-tat way. You have to love their friends coming over if you ever want to have your friends around. This lie is also a good bargaining chip for the future: "I let you have your friends over!" or "I love your friends!" are two statements (the latter probably a lie) that make you look good in any tough spot. Friends are a big issue within relationships and they are often harder to cope with than relatives or children.

※ ※ ※

"No, what you were saying is more interesting than what I was watching."—You know you are grateful for your partner. You love them. Where would you be without them? But do they have to talk when you are reading, watching TV, listening to music, have the radio on, or are merely staring out the window dreaming of a new life? The problem with relationships is that they are demanding. Like any working bit of machinery, they need oiling and maintainence. And talking is part of it. Wanting to give something else your attention is selfish, slovenly, and hurtful. Once you are in a relationship, your private air space is no longer your own. ❀

HOWARD WHO?

Tycoon Howard Hughes had been the world's most famous recluse for 15 years. In 1972 he decided to tell all in his autobiography. The man who had secured the publishing scoop of the century was American Clifford Irving. Armed with a tape recorder, he spent months in discussion with Hughes, going over his life in a series of secret meetings in Mexico and the Bahamas. And Hughes had certainly led the kind of life that makes good copy—a potent mix of big business, even bigger money, and big planes (the giant flying boat nicknamed the *Spruce Goose*). As well as his daredevil pioneer aviation exploits, in the 1930s and '40s when Hollywood was at its most glamorous, Hughes had squired a seemingly endless list of beautiful film stars. Add to this the public's prurient interest in the rumors surrounding Hughes's later years [??] and his voluntary incarceration in a succession of darkened hotel rooms, plus some very weird personal habits [??]. It just couldn't go wrong. Irving approached major publishers McGraw Hill, with whom he had already worked. Convinced by his story of being commissioned by Hughes and the letters supporting his claim, McGraw Hill were happy to publish what would undoubtedly be a huge best-seller.

Irving managed to broker a deal that netted an astronomical $750,000 as an advance. However, shortly before publication, a furious Hughes called *Time Life* reporter Frank McCulloch to expose the fraud. McCulloch didn't know what to think. After all, Hughes could be dead for all anybody knew. He decided to read the manuscript and, finding it surprisingly accurate, concluded that the call must have been a hoax. Finding no action had been taken as a result of his call, Hughes organized a telephone meeting with 7 other reporters. Speaking publicly for the first time in years he said, "I only wish I were still in the movie business, because I don't remember any script as wild or as stretching the imagination as this yarn has turned out to be."

The whole thing had been fabricated by Irving, whose audacity had been quite awe inspiring. He had even gone so far as to forge correspondence with Hughes in which the book deal was discussed, and fabricate legal documents that backed it all up. Lured into a false sense of security by Hughes's long silence, Irving had assumed that even if he was still alive he would not break his super-reclusive habit of 15 years by speaking to anyone in the outside world, let alone the press. Irving protested his innocence and even went so far as to do so on TV. But he had lied about his movements. His travel records did not match up with the times he said that he and his tape recorder had been having a one-to-one with Hughes. To make matters worse, his Danish girlfriend, Baroness Nina van Pallandt, confirmed that he had been with her when he said he was in Mexico. The investigative reporter James Phelan produced more hard evidence when he was able to show that Irving had pinched a part of Phelan's own unpublished book on Hughes. Irving had been backed into a corner. The printing presses were stopped and Irving got 2 and a half years for his pains. However, the book finally did see the light of day, although not until 27 years later. In 1999, *Clifford Irving's Autobiography of Howard Hughes* was finally published by Terrific Books. ✎

BANNED IN THE MIDDLE EAST

In several Middle Eastern countries it is forbidden for filmmakers to show a character listening to music and ironing a pair of pants at the same time. Apparently it encourages children to be rude to their parents. 💾💣

TOP SEX LIES

1. Size doesn't matter.
2. Douching with Pepsi Cola is a reliable form of contraception.
3. You can't catch a sexually transmitted disease if it is your first time having sex.
4. Clingfilm makes an effective condom.
5. Excess alcohol helps your sexual performance and stamina.
6. Thinking of the World Series helps.
7. It's never happened to me before.
8. Of course I won't tell anyone.
9. A man can tell when a woman is faking it.
10. You can catch STDs from toilet seats.
11. Gynecologists make better lovers.
12. To give is as good as to receive. 💾💣

TOP 11 PROFESSIONAL LIE DETECTORS

Most of us are hopeless at spotting liars: we get it right only 44 percent of the time, which is less than chance. Some professions rely on people who have excellent lie-detecting skills, including:

1. Police officers
2. Forensic psychiatrists
3. Clinical psychologists
4. Private investigators
5. FBI agents
6. Customs officials
7. Immigration officials
8. Lawyers
9. Judges
10. Social workers
11. Parole officers 📖

RAY CHARLES REGAINED HIS SIGHT IN 1984

But he carried on pretending to be blind so he could grope women with total impunity. 💾💧

LEMMINGS ARE SUICIDAL

Despite popular opinion, nature is not, after all, so whimsical as to make lemmings suicidal, whether to regulate numbers or otherwise. The blame for this lie can be placed firmly at the door of the Disney corporation. The lie is born of the truth that lemmings migrate en masse, and when they do so and are unfamiliar with the lay of the land, the occasional casualty results.

Enter the 1958 Disney nature documentary *White Wilderness*, filmed in Alberta, Canada, and featuring a few lemmings bought from Inuit children. Researchers urged their lemmings to jump off a snow-covered turntable and, most memorably and unethically of all, to jump off a river cliff. ⌛

TOP 10 ROCK LIES #2

1. There is anything deep about any of U2's lyrics.
2. Alexander O'Neal once sweated so much on stage that his clothes disintegrated.
3. Charles Manson auditioned for The Monkees.
4. Robert Plant was once an accountant.
5. Colonel Tom Parker, Elvis's manager, was ever in the army.
6. Snoop Dogg is gay.
7. The song "Mr. Tambourine Man" is about drugs.
8. The song "Perfect Day" *isn't* about drugs.
9. The song "Lucy in the Sky with Diamonds" is about anybody called Lucy.
10. Ice-T was once a gangsta. 🖥️🌑

14 TIMES A LADY

History is full of tales about men who have married duplicitly. Most often these men were bigamists, but occasionally they were married as the bride, often with the husband never suspecting that he'd married a man, even after several years of conjugal bliss.

History is less full of tales about women who have married as men, though. Yet Mary Hamilton managed to convince fourteen women that she was a man and married them as Charles, George, or William Hamilton. That is until 1746 when Mary's final victim, Mary Price, finally began to suspect that she might have been short changed in the husband stakes. Mary Price told the court at the Quarter Sessions in Somerset that they had "bedded and lived together as man and wife for more than a quarter of a year." Clearly in a state of some confusion, the court's verdict was, "we sentence her, or him, whichever he or she may be, to be imprisoned six months, and during that time to be whipped in the towns of Taunton, Glastonbury, Wells, and Shepton Mallet." 🖎

LIES IN QUOTES

ROUND NUMBERS ARE
ALWAYS FALSE.
Dr. Samuel Johnson (1709–1784)

A LIE CAN TRAVEL HALFWAY
ROUND THE WORLD WHILE THE
TRUTH IS PUTTING ON ITS
SHOES.
Mark Twain (1835–1910)

OF COURSE I LIE TO PEOPLE,
BUT I LIE ALTRUISTICALLY—FOR
OUR MUTUAL GOOD. THE LIE IS
THE BASIC BUILDING BLOCK OF
GOOD MANNERS.
Quentin Crisp (1908–1999)

ANY FOOL CAN TELL THE TRUTH,
BUT IT REQUIRES A MAN OF
SOME SENSE TO KNOW HOW TO
LIE WELL.
Samuel Butler (1835–1902)

I HAVE BEEN THINKING THAT I
WOULD MAKE A PROPOSITION
TO MY REPUBLICAN FRIENDS . . .
THAT IF THEY WILL STOP TELLING
LIES ABOUT THE DEMOCRATS, WE
WILL STOP TELLING THE TRUTH
ABOUT THEM.
Adlai Stevenson (1900–1965)

A LITTLE INACCURACY
SOMETIMES SAVES TONS OF
EXPLANATION.
Saki (1870–1916)

WHITE LIES ALWAYS INTRODUCE
OTHERS OF A DARKER
COMPLEXION.
William Paley (1743–1805)

O, WHAT A TANGLED WEB WE
WEAVE WHEN FIRST WE
PRACTICE TO DECEIVE!
Sir Walter Scott (1771–1832)

A LIE IS AN ABOMINATION UNTO
THE LORD AND A VERY PRESENT
HELP IN TROUBLE.
Adlai Stevenson (1900–1965)

NO MAN HAS A GOOD ENOUGH
MEMORY TO MAKE A
SUCCESSFUL LIAR.
Abraham Lincoln (1809–1865)

THE LIAR'S PUNISHMENT IS NOT
IN THE LEAST THAT HE IS NOT
BELIEVED, BUT THAT HE
CANNOT BELIEVE ANYONE ELSE.
George Bernard Shaw (1856–1950)

IN HUMAN RELATIONSHIPS,
KINDNESS AND LIES ARE WORTH
A THOUSAND TRUTHS.
Graham Greene (1904–1991)

REPETITION DOES NOT TURN A
LIE INTO A TRUTH.
Franklin D. Roosevelt (1882–1945)

ROCK MYTHS EXPLODED #3

SOUL SINGER JACKIE WILSON WAS A BOXING CHAMPION.
Actually, he wasn't. His record company publicists were largely responsible for the story that the singer had been a Golden Gloves champion before he started recording. He had been a boxer, but during his brief career as a professional he won only 2 fights out of 10 and got beaten so badly in the last of them that he sought alternative employment.

MICHAEL JACKSON'S *THRILLER* IS THE BIGGEST SELLING
ALBUM OF ALL TIME.
At the time of writing (Spring 2005) it had sold 26 million, but, according to the RIAA (Recording Industry Association of America), it was overtaken some time in 2003 by The Eagles's *Their Greatest Hits*, which has, to date, sold 28 million.

BOBBY DARIN AND FRANK SINATRA HATED EACH OTHER.
Sure there was a professional rivalry, but never the personal loathing so beloved of gossip columnists. In fact, the two singers had a great deal of mutual respect.

"THE ADVENTURES OF GRANDMASTER FLASH ON THE WHEELS OF
STEEL" WAS THE FIRST SINGLE TO QUICK-MIX OTHER TUNES
(BEARING IN MIND THE SUGARHILL GANG WERE BACKED BY A COVER
VERSION-PROFICIENT BAND FOR "RAPPER'S DELIGHT").
Enterprising souls had been splicing together bits of other records for 50 years before Flash's hit, with the first known example being The Happiness Boys' "Twisting the Dial" in 1928, which did a good job of simulating a radio dial being surfed.

STEAMBOAT PRESIDENT

Walt Disney Productions have an open-ended agreement with the United Nations that Mickey Mouse will never run for the Presidency of the United States. This is because surveys have shown the cartoon rodent would win by a landslide and other member countries wouldn't want to host state visits from either him or Pluto (his obvious VP).

LIES MEN TELL WOMEN #2

"I don't mind romantic comedies. You know that." Every man hates rom-coms because they are blueprints to the end of their happy existence. They not only give women unreasonable expectations, but they also pander to the worst things romance can offer: unremitting loving devotion from good-looking men.

※   ※   ※

"I only had two beers."—Lie. He is pretending not to know how to count. What he means is that he had two beers with Tony, then went and had two more with Simon then bumped into Brendan and had two more. Since he's forgotten that he met the other two men, it seems to him that he has only, in fact, had two beers in total. Next time, he will count the Aboriginal way where he can only count to six and after that the rest are "many." You don't need to know how many beers he's had really. He can't stand up so he's had more than enough.

※   ※   ※

"I wasn't looking at her, I thought I knew the man next to her."—Total lie. She's good looking, a stranger, and he was fantasizing about her when you caught him. That's the meaning behind these weasel words. He's a man, he has to look, much in the same way as if he'd bought the car of his dreams and still looks in the dealer's window. He's shopping. Let him shop. Just don't give him a credit card, car keys, or time off for good behavior. Meanwhile, check out the guy next to the girl in case you need to play the game as well.

※   ※   ※

"Alison? Alison was my cat!"—A man needs to cover his verbal mistakes and sometimes a lie is the only way to do it. When caught saying the wrong name at the wrong time, a man may have to resort to a lie which, as he sees it, saves hard feelings all around. If he said another woman's name, it doesn't mean he was actually thinking you were her. He may, after all, just be thinking how much nicer she is and how he wishes he were with her rather than you. That's all. Nothing to be concerned about here.

※   ※   ※

"Sure, I'd love to talk."—Such a lie! No man likes to talk unless he's had too many espressos or if he has a joke book open at his favorite page. But he will talk to make you like him. Of course, you may notice that talking for him is mostly listening to you. That is as it should be. Any man who opens himself up for a chat knows what he is getting into: yards of words with possibly some sex or food when the torrent is over. Or maybe he'll get to take a nap or watch some sports. Either way, he'll get a reward and feel like a good person. But liking it? He'll never like it.

※　※　※

"No, you're not fat."—A lie of sorts. A man rarely cares what a woman looks like until he starts to think about not liking her. Men don't care about body shape as much as women do, although each one will have the type he likes. (This is why your man will never go for a supermodel unless you happen to be a supermodel.) Men like peace and quiet. If they wanted to know the truth about their body, they'd go to a specialist. They wouldn't ask their partner. But they know what you want to hear—and they are, in the interests of an Easy Life, more than willing to give it to you. ❀

MODERN MASTERS DONE CHEAP

The art world has known forgers almost as long as it has existed. There have been many successful forgers over the past 2 millennia, but there have been few as expert in lying about his art and provenance as John Myatt.

Myatt made a name for himself as an art forger with the paintings he faked for fellow Briton and art dealer John Drewe at the end of the 20th century. Myatt put an ad in the satirical magazine *Private Eye* offering to paint fake works by 19th- and 20th-century artists for modest sums. Myatt was being totally upfront about the nature of his paintings. They would be sold as acknowledged fakes to decorate the homes and offices of those who hankered after the real thing but couldn't possibly afford it. As a result of the ad, he was contacted by John Drewe who claimed that Myatt's work would fit the bill perfectly. He was a fine arts fan and wanted some pictures for his own home. However, in reality Drewe was an art dealer, a role that enabled him to sell one of Myatt's Albert Gleizes paintings to Christie's for £25,000.

Clearly for that kind of money Christie's were under the impression that it was the genuine article, but Myatt was yet another talented artist who could mimic the style of many of the modern masters. As well as Gleizes, he imitated such painters as Alberto Giacometti, Marc Chagall, Matisse, Graham Sutherland, and Nicholas de Stael. Myatt's own particular recipe for an authentic-looking paint finish was an interesting combination of emulsion paint and K-Y Jelly, aged with vacuum cleaner dust and dirt.

Myatt went on to paint some 200 forgeries in total for Drewe, which Drewe sold to collectors and top auction houses all over the world. In 1995, some of the fakes were eventually traced to Myatt who confessed readily and, ashamed of his part in the scam, offered to return some of the money that he had been paid. He was also ready to point the finger at Drewe, with whom he had fallen out. Drewe was arrested in 1996 when the police raided his gallery and found equipment used to forge certificates of authenticity and other back-up documents. He had managed to gain access to the archives at some of London's top museums, enabling him to create convincing provenance for the forgeries. Both men were convicted of conspiracy to defraud and were sentenced. Myatt got 1 year, although he only served 4 months, and, though he claimed he had been made a scapegoat, Drewe got 6 years, of which he served 2. Of the 200 or so forgeries the Myatt/Drewe partnership unleashed on the world, the police managed to track down just 70 or so, which means there are still quite a few out there. Released from prison a free and chastened man, Myatt continued his painting, both acknowledged copies of the masters and commissioned portraits, and even exhibited under his own name. ✎

ANIMAL LIES OR TRUTH #3

Lie: Spiders' webs are all the same.
Truth: To us. They are as individual and as unique to the spider who spins them as a finger print is to humans.

Lie: Pythons and boa constrictors literally crush their prey to death.
Truth: Once it has breathed out, they will suffocate the prey by constricting its body so it can't breath in again.

Lie: Horses can be trained to "dance" in time to music.

Truth: In circuses the band will be good enough to play in time to whatever the horse feels like doing.

Lie: When thousands of fish in a shoal apparently maneuver simultaneously, at speed, they are obeying a command from one squadron leader fish.
Truth: They are merely reacting to what the fish nearest to them are doing. Their reaction is so quick, though, that they all appear to be doing it at the same time. ▣

BIG DOT/LITTLE DOT ILLUSION

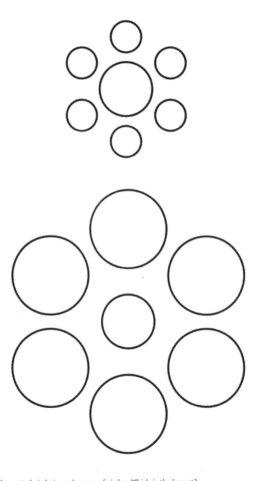

Look at the central circle in each group of circles. Which is the largest?

CROP CIRCLES ARE MADE BY ALIENS

Using their spaceships and not by drunken idiots with too much time on their
hands and long planks tied on to their feet. 🖫◆

AN OFFICER AND A COBBLER

In Prussian Berlin in 1906 military men were much admired and the military above reproach from civilians. Which was a great help to 60-something diminutive cobbler and small-time crook Wilhelm Voigt.

Having purchased a second-hand captain's uniform, he commandeered a squad of grenadiers who had just been relieved of guard duty and made for the town hall of Köpenick, a suburb of Berlin. He entered the building with the soldiers and proceeded to arrest the mayor and his staff on the grounds of suspected embezzlement and confiscated 4,000 marks from the town coffers. Once outside, Voigt ordered the soldiers to march the mayor and his staff under guard to Berlin's military headquarters while he made off with the money, discarding the uniform and sword along the way.

Unfortunately for him though, Voigt was not at liberty for long. The military needed to save face and so tracked him down just over a week later and he was given a 4-year jail sentence.

The German public however made something of a folk-hero out of Voigt, and pressured the kaiser to pardon him after just 2 years of his sentence. Once free, he capitalized on his celebrity by donning a captain's uniform again, this time to recount his exploits on the music hall stage as Captain von Köpenick. He was even immortalized in wax in London's Madame Tussauds. ✎

THE EAGLES'S *HOTEL CALIFORNIA* WAS WRITTEN AS A TRIBUTE TO LUCIFER

Astonishingly, when the song came out in 1976, Christian groups in America put together a strong case for the prosecution. They claimed lines such as "kill the beast" and "you can check out any time you like but you can never leave" were obvious nods to Satanism, while lyrics about the spirit of 1969 were clearly meant to refer to the publishing of the first Satanic Bible, the Manson murders, and the Stones's catastrophic Altamont concert, all of which occurred during that year. But the clincher, they maintained, was the spooky figure with the neatly trimmed goatee beard lurking in the background of the cover photo—clearly Mephistophelian imagery. Not according to lyricist Don Henley: the song was never more than a send-up of L.A. excess, and the character on the sleeve was a technician standing in the wrong place and nobody noticed. 🖫

DANGER IN HOLLYWOOD

It might be a fantasy land, but some things are just too fantastical to believe . . .

In the very distant background of a scene in *The Wizard of Oz*, you can see an extra who is playing a Munchkin committing suicide by hanging himself.

Six extras were killed during filming of the chariot race in *Ben-Hur*.

Steve Martin was murdered in 1988, during the making of *Parenthood*, by a sinister group of Hollywood producers who believed the comedian was out of control. He was replaced by a look-a-like who believed *Father of the Bride* and *Housesitter* were funny.

Will Smith was abducted during the making of *I Robot*, but his superstar demands, while being held captive, were such that his kidnappers couldn't afford to keep him. They gave him back before the movie's production company and Smith's wife could scrape together the ransom. 🖫🌢

YOU WILL GET UPGRADED TO BUSINESS CLASS ON A FLIGHT IF . . .

You are wearing a suit and handing out business cards. 🖫🌢

HOW TO GET AWAY WITH LYING

As Freud said, "No mortal can keep a secret. If his lips are silent, he chatters with his fingertips. Betrayal oozes out of him at every pore." Freud thought that we give ourselves away by our facial expressions, tone of voice, and body language. And many of us do, but there are those among us who have worked hard at lying so convincingly that they show no trace of their deception. However, it seems that in certain cases, you could wear a T-shirt stating "I'm a Liar!" and get away with it. Studies published at the beginning of the 21st century show that in some circumstances people are more easily deceived than in others—no matter how you behave. But to improve your chances of passing off a lie undetected you should:

BE ATTRACTIVE.

We tend to have stereotypical responses to attractive people, believing they are more friendly, likeable, intelligent, trustworthy, and honest. Attractive people are less likely to be found guilty of criminal behavior—perhaps because juries and judges instinctively believe they are more credible and honest than less attractive people and so don't look for the same content or facial "cues" that suggest they are lying. Studies show that self-confident, attractive people are also more fluent liars under pressure—perhaps because they perceive they will be believed.

BE THE SAME SEX AS THE PERSON YOU ARE TRYING TO CONVINCE.

Women think women are more honest than men; men think men are more honest than women. Psychologists believe this gender bias is due to our stereotypical conditioning about the opposite sex.

DO IT OVER THE PHONE.

You're more likely to get caught out lying when people can see your face and read your facial expressions, than when they can just hear the content and tone of what you're saying. So to be sure of lying successfully to the IRS (not that you should, of course), only deal with them over the telephone.

DO IT TO SOMEONE WHO IS SOCIALLY ANXIOUS.

Nervous people are less likely to notice a person is lying, perhaps because their focus is on their own social worries, rather than on assessing those around them.

DON'T CARE TOO MUCH.

Those who are highly motivated to deceive—for example, someone trying to convince a partner that they are not having an affair—are more easily caught out lying than those who don't care as much about the outcome. 📖

BOOK BLURB LIES #3

"Insightful"

Won't tell you anything you don't already know. The author of this book has written about what he or she thinks about—lint, dust bunnies, mortgage payments. There's nothing really insightful about it. The author isn't "seeing into the nature of things" unless the book is about microbiology. Insights do not mean inner dialog.

"Memorable"

Or, for those who like short words, the same as "will stay with you long after the last page is turned." You'll feel as if you've wasted your time reading this and it will take you days to figure out why—and, in fact, why you ever picked the book up in the first place.

"On acid"

Should have been good but isn't and yet we need to publish something. This phrase is taken from the once-fashionable style of gonzo writing as practiced by Hunter S. Thompson, even if he would probably never use the term "on acid." Unfortunately, his talent and free style influenced generations of writers who couldn't handle the gonzo style, thereby running it into the ground.

"Remarkable"

A clever use of a good word that means, "worthy of being or likely to be noticed especially as being uncommon or extraordinary." So this is a book which is not quite unique but, somehow, in an ineffable sort of way, worth being looked at, bought, read, and then thrown across the room whereupon you will notice it.

"Revealing"

A word that seems to project the notion of inside information, e.g., a tell-all about the plumbing industry as told by a real plumber. The author, one thinks, has a special relationship to his or her subject. Perhaps they are writing about their famous mother, knowing Howard Hughes, or being one of the many women who wrote fan letters to Mel Gibson after *The Year Of Living Dangerously*. Revealing, in its ordinary use, means nothing more than what the author is thinking—and the author is thinking that he or she should have hung out in more pool halls than libraries.

"Searing"

Not the culinary skill of heating something to the point where the exterior is burned shut. Rather, this is used as in a "searing statement" that could be "searingly brutal." What is searing? No one really knows, but it is fairly serious and as close to bad as you can get when it comes to commenting on someone or something. It is almost damning something, that's how bad it is. You can't get sued for "searing," though.

"Shining through"

The book could be written better, perhaps by someone else. And we've published it. So we're stuck really. If you look closely, there are a few glimmers of what we really wanted this book to be, without our support and marketing and editing, naturally. Within this book, you'll find a few nice things. And these nice things "shine through" the fact that you'll probably end up giving this book to Goodwill.

"Sprawling"

This is not *Gone with the Wind*. It is much longer. In fact, it spreads out when other books have daintily held themselves in. This is usually used when the author is far too generous with either temporal or spatial description. This does not mean the book lost its balance and could hardly stand although that term may be perfectly applicable to its author.

"Sports or wears his/her erudition lightly"

We've found an academic whose sense of humor hasn't been squeezed out of them by the "publish or perish" rules of tenured life. This is usually attributed to someone who either already wrote an academic tome, only to see it sink beneath the waves of the book market, or someone who may actually have time to read something other than their chosen subject. Being able to be a showoff with everything you know and not have your readers hate you is a rare thing indeed. ✾

HOW TO FIND A LIAR

Log on to findaliar.com, a website founded in 2004 by Amber Didreckson. A single mother of 2, Ms. Didreckson started the site because in her search for a legitimate work-at-home opportunity, she encountered many liars, cheats, scammers, retired attorneys, and generally very, very, bad people. After many hours wasted, dollars spent, and a lawsuit, she realized she wasn't alone. She discovered a research strategy she uses for herself and to forewarn others about the bad opportunities before they waste time and money looking for ways to support their families. 📖

A PENGUIN LIE

Penguins are magnetic. That's why they congregate at the South Pole. Any penguins that escape from a zoo in the Northern Hemisphere gradually migrate to the North Pole. However, the Coriolis Effect in the northern hemisphere makes them go round in circles on their way north, so they can't run away from polar bears. Being social creatures and communicative, too, over the past 1,000 years news has been handed down through generations of penguins that if in doubt, head South. Of course, not all make it, though, which pleases some polar bears, at least. 📖🩸

THE 3 MOST COMMONLY USED LIES IN THE WORLD

I love you
The check is in the mail (or, I'll check with accounts)
I'll be there in 5 minutes 📖

THE PRESIDENT'S LIES

BILL CLINTON

I want you to listen to me. I'm not going to say this again, I did not have sexual
relations with that woman—Miss Lewinsky. I never told anyone to lie, not a
single time . . . never. These accusations are false. And I need to get back to work
for the American people.

*The president responds to accusations of sexual infidelity in the White House, 26
January 1998. In August 1998 he would admit that, "I did have a relationship
with Miss Lewinsky that was not appropriate. In fact it was wrong."* 📖

CAN 2,070,000 LIES BE WRONG?

A Google search for the phrase "Bush lies" on 11 September 2004 produced
2,070,000 results within 0.23 seconds. Among them were 3 websites that used
the phrase as their domain name—bushlies.com, bushlies.net, and bush-
lies.blogspot.com—with another 5 that had substantial pages on the subject.
They were bushwatch.org/bushlies, bush.tvnewslies.org,
cafepress.com/sgbushlies, highway4.org/bush_lies, and
georgewalkerbush.net/toptenlies. 📖

TRUE LIES #69,666

Elvis Presley is dead. However, he did not die of natural causes. He was
assassinated by U.S. Special Services in revenge for the death of John F.
Kennedy. Elvis had ordered the shooting of JFK because he believed that the
former U.S. president had ordered the CIA to kill Marilyn Monroe. Elvis was killed
by CIA black operatives to celebrate the 30th anniversary of the founding of the
CIA. 📖🔪

EXPLODING FOOD MYTHS

THE OLDER A BOTTLE OF WINE, THE BETTER IT WILL BE.

The enormous majority of wine should be drunk as soon into its life as possible, so as to best experience the fruit flavors—after 6 months the taste will start to diminish. At most, the very best 10 percent of red and 5 percent of white will improve if left in the bottle, and for the majority of them that will only be for the first year; then it will only be about 10 percent of these wines that will go on getting better and that improvement will very rarely continue after 10 years.

ORGANIC CROPS WILL BE COMPLETELY FREE FROM CHEMICAL PESTICIDES.

There are so many chemicals flying about the rural atmosphere from farms that spray their crops, it is unlikely that airborne particulates are not settling on organic farms. However, it will be a lot less than if they were sprayed on purpose.

FRUIT FLAVOR.

If it's written like that—as opposed to fruit flavor*ed*—it doesn't have to ever have had any contact with the fruit concerned; the best you can hope for is that it tastes something like it. The latter, with the "ed," would have to have been flavored with the genuine fruit.

MARGARINE IS HEALTHIER THAN BUTTER.
The process of making margarine can create trans fats, which the body has no way of processing and so will hang around in your system doing relatively far more damage than the fat in butter. Trans fats are a result of setting margarine into a solid block, so the softer it is the less trans fats it will contain and the healthier it will be.

ALL CHOLESTEROL IS BAD AND SHOULD BE AVOIDED.
Cholesterol is a vital part of the make up of the body's cells, and it's only when it's present in excess it can become troublesome, and then not always. There are two forms, High Density Lipoprotein (HDL) and Low Density Lipoprotein (LDL). Any excess of the former is taken to the liver for reprocessing, while the latter hangs around to clog up the arteries. Unfortunately, when eating cholesterol rich food, you have no idea which type will be formed in your system. 💾

20 LIES WE ALL TELL

I won't tell a soul

Traffic was terrible

I thought that was next week

Your hair looks great

You've lost some weight

I couldn't eat another thing

There will never be another you

I'll never get over you

I turned the boss down on that

I don't want your money

That's not mine

I was going to get a bigger car but I'm worried about the Greenhouse effect

I voted for George W. Bush

I didn't inhale

I never said that

Sorry, I don't have any change

It was a bargain

I've never faked it

I didn't see you there

I never lie 📖

MORE ROCK LIES

The Beastie Boys would base
their entire international touring
schedule around the snowboarding
season in different parts of
the world.

Pink Floyd built the Berlin Wall.

Barry White weighed 150 lbs, but
wore a fat suit every time he left his
house because his public expected
him to be fat.

Sam & Dave liked each other.

Prince composed his songs for the
1989 film *Batman* while hanging
upside down in the dark.

The Tommy Lee/Pamela
Anderson sex video was personal
and never meant to see the light
of day. 🖥📱

LEARNED LYING #2: ACADEMICS

As anyone who has ever been to university can tell you, just because what you're
being told is in the form of an aphorism, doesn't mean that it's the truth. Neither
should the fact that you do not understand a word's original meaning get in the way
of your knowing when you are being lied to by professors or professional smart-alecks.
Here are just some smart words and phrases that have been used in the pursuit of
the untruth.

BIFURCATION
MEANING
Offering 2 alternatives to a situation
when there are, in fact, more; e.g.,
"Either you give me your money or I
take it. That's your choice." Problem
with use: Two isn't a big number. Most
people could think of alternatives
fairly easily.

FALLACY OF INTERROGATION
MEANING
Asking a question that presupposed
the answer; e.g., "So, how long have
you been stealing money from my wallet?" Problem with use: Entails a
lengthy amount of time for denial. Can
be boring.

FALSE ANALOGY
MEANING
Using similarity where it shouldn't be
used; e.g., "You have money from my
wallet so me stealing from your wallet
is okay." Problem with use: Works well
unless used on smart people.

PLURIUM INTERROGATIONUM
MEANING

Wanting a simple answer to a question that can't really have a simple answer; e.g., "So, when did you stop beating your wife and then offering me money to say you didn't do it? Answer yes or no!" Problem with use: Is more amusing than effective.

NON-SEQUITUR
MEANING

Using something that doesn't follow from your argument to prove something else; e.g., "Everyone has a wallet like yours. Why would I, then, want to take money from it?" Problem with use: Demands keeping track of many details and knowing where you are going with your lie.

RED HERRING
MEANING

Using something to divert attention away from your argument; e.g., "I did not take money from your wallet— but I may know a person who did!" Problem with use: Must be employed judiciously and quickly, otherwise you may be pursued by locals with pitchforks and torches.

REIFICATION
MEANING

Transforming an abstract thing into something concrete; e.g., "I used your credit to buy cement. There." Problem with use: Many people don't see money, their wives, their husbands, their cars, or other things you may wish to lie about as "abstract" objects. Even Picassos don't count.

SHIFT THE BURDEN OF PROOF
MEANING

Making someone else responsible for the truth of your statement; e.g., "I did not take your wallet. Ask that woman over there." Problem with use: Does cause suspicion unless used wisely.

SPECIAL PLEADING
MEANING

Asking for special treatment; e.g., "I may or may not have taken your money from your wallet but I am only a simple person with slender fingers and I ask you not to judge me too harshly. In fact, I think I'll just run off right now because I need to." Problem with use: Won't work with really important, anger-making lies. Little lies, it works very well with.

STRAW MAN
MEANING

Putting up a defense only to knock it down for show; e.g., "Of course, I may have taken your wallet if I were a poor, naked, shivering wreck just climbing out of the river, soaking wet, and, finding that I needed money, chanced upon your wallet with the notes bulging out of it . . ." Problem with use: May dazzle those whom you are trying to fool if used elegantly. ❀

FIRST EDITIONS FORGERY

This deception was made particularly intriguing by the several eminent names attached to it.

It was the 1930s and two London booksellers, John Carter and Graham Pollard, decided to get together to solve a particularly knotty literary problem. Written evidence, including a biography of Ruskin, suggested that there existed rare, valuable pamphlets by certain Victorian writers, but through Carter and Pollard's knowledge of the authors and the pamphlets themselves it soon emerged that something was not right.

In the case of the Ruskin pamphlets, the problem was that they were meant to be first editions, but they contained later, revised Ruskin text. A "first edition" pamphlet of Elizabeth Barrett Browning's *Sonnets from the Portuguese* was printed in Reading, but the Brownings were in fact living in Italy in 1847, the time it was published. Why had the Brownings not therefore taken the logical step and used an Italian printer? The literary critic Edmund Gosse said that he had heard from a friend that E. B. B.'s friend Mary Russell Mitford had arranged for the printing. It was said that Mitford had held on to some of those pamphlets and they had since been sold to collectors for $1,250 each.

In the course of their research into the Elizabeth Barrett Browning pamphlets, Carter and Pollard were informed by bibliographer Thomas J. Wise that the pamphlets had been passed from Mitford on to another friend of hers who sold them on to Browning collectors.

Two types of analysis showed that this story did not hang together. Analysis of the paper showed that the pamphlets were made from wood pulp, which had only been used from the 1840s; analysis of the lettering showed the font used was one that had not emerged until the 1880s.

The booksellers were by now satisfied that several pamphlets were "wrong"; all that remained was to establish who the forger was. The printers of the pamphlets were Clay and Son, who when questioned by detectives explained that a fire in 1911 had destroyed all their records. This meant that the commissioner of the Elizabeth Barrett Browning pamphlets could not be established. The booksellers found a lot of other forged pamphlets, by authors including George Eliot, Tennyson, and Matthew Arnold. In each case the title page of the document would contain information explaining its early publication.

So could Wise be the unnamed friend of Gosse? Certainly they knew each other, but he was so respected. . . . On the other hand, Wise had sold hundreds of forged pamphlets to innocent antiquarian bookseller Herbert Gorfin, and Wise's connections with Browning societies would have placed him perfectly for such a scam. When questioned years before about a couple of forged first editions, Wise had accused two other literary types, both dead. By the time Carter and Pollard got to Wise he was 73 and exploiting this fact for all it was worth. He was vague and said he had a bad memory, but, he said, he would try and find records of the Gorfin sales. They never did receive those records.

There cannot be much doubt about Wise's guilt. Shortly after Carter and Pollard visited him, he offered Gorfin £400 for any pamphlets still in his possession and asked him to say he had bought them from Buxton Forman, another esteemed bibliographer. Forman was also dead by this time but he had known Wise and further research revealed that he might well have been involved in the forgeries in some more marginal way. Gorfin took

the money but would not participate in the lie about Forman. Wise maintained in letters to the *Times Literary Supplement* that Forman was behind the pamphlets. He died in 1937 still protesting his innocence.

In an interesting twist to the tale, collectors since Wise's time have become interested in forgeries and forgers as collectors' items in and of themselves. One such is Frank W. Tober, whose Wise forgeries formed the element of his library that he most prized. When he died in 1995, he bequeathed his entire collection to the University of Delaware. ⧗

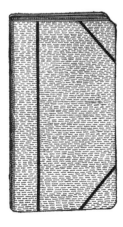

BEATLES LIES

More than any other popular music artists, The Beatles excited numerous rumors, myths, and downright untruths about them. Here are 5 of the more entertaining:

John Lennon wrote the lyrics to "Eleanor Rigby."
In spite of what he was given to "mischievously" tell people in interview, they were always Paul's words.

Paul McCartney died in 1966.
In September 1969 an Illinois student magazine ran a story that McCartney had been dead for three years following a car crash in Scotland and the current left-handed bass player was a lookalike. A Detroit radio station picked up the story and by October it was "fact," with an American Beatles fanzine reinterpreting the group's visuals to offer a series of compelling "evidence" to the hushed-up demise, including: in the background of the fadeout of "Strawberry Fields Forever," John is heard to chant "I buried Paul, I buried Paul"; Paul wearing an armband reading OPD on the front of the Sgt. Pepper sleeve—Officially Pronounced Dead—and Paul looking away from the camera on the back of that sleeve; Paul sitting under a sign reading "I was" in the Magical Mystery Tour booklet; and so on. But the most blatant clue was the Abbey Road sleeve: the procession across the crosswalk apparently represented Paul's funeral—George is dressed as a gravedigger, Ringo an undertaker, and John as a priest, while Paul has bare feet which, in some Eastern cultures, signifies he has been prepared for burial. The clincher is the car in the background with the number plate 28IF—Paul would have been 28 if he was still alive.

The Beatles smoked a joint in the toilets at Buckingham Palace before they received their MBE's in 1965.
They didn't. They had a cigarette.

The Beatles's classic "You've Got to Hide Your Love Away" was written by John Lennon to manager Brian Epstein after they had a brief gay fling.
No, it wasn't.

The group Silkie, who had a Top 10 hit with "You've Got to Hide Your Love Away" in the U.S. in 1965, were The Beatles under an alias.
Not quite: George played guitar on the track, Paul played tambourine, and John produced it. 🖫

PERSPECTIVE ILLUSION

Above: Are all of the figures the same size, or do they get bigger the farther from you they are?

DIET LIES #2

YOU CAN EAT ALL YOU WANT BEFORE 5 OR 7 P.M. AND LOSE WEIGHT: No, you can't change the order in which you eat food and lose weight, although many diets would have you believe this malicious food lie. Merely cutting off food at the end of your day won't make a weight loss if you are making up for *not* eating during the day. This is the food equivalent of someone saying, "I rode my bike around the corner so I can now have ice cream." Unless that corner is the actual corner of Nebraska, you haven't burned off enough calories to warrant a scoop of ice cream. Not eating after 5 or 7 P.M. in the evening can also mean you wake up ravenous and gulp down more calories at breakfast than you would normally. If the evening is when you tend to wolf down the largest portion of your daily caloric intake, then this rule could help you lose weight.

EAT ONLY GREEN AND WHITE THINGS:

What starts out as a promising dietary rule turns out to be fraught with the problem of the dietary lie: for starters, green and white are also colors of jelly beans, beer bottles, cake, cookies, candies, and many other calorie-rich items which, frankly, are designed as occasional food. The green and white diet does work if you make the green and white things vegetables and fish. Sticking to the green and

white diet will eventually deplete your body of much-needed nutrients. Sure, if you have to lose weight for an occasion (holiday, wedding, reunion) eating like this will work provided you don't cheat. So that means no fried green tomatoes, no vanilla ice cream, etc. The only way green and white is right is if it was called The Eat Only Steamed Plain Green Vegetable and Steamed White Fish and Nothing Else for a Week Diet.

TO LOSE WEIGHT, DO NOT MIX STARCH AND PROTEIN AT THE SAME MEAL:

The famous food combining diet is purported to work on a scientific study of human digestion. The trouble is, as with most diets based on such statements, the experts are not in agreement on this point. Merely avoiding eating, say, a meat sandwich will not cause you to lose weight unless you eat far too many of them on a daily basis. If food combining helps with weight loss it is because eating vegetables and meat without any starch (bread, rice, potatoes, etc.) is extremely boring. One can only eat so much of such a combination and even then moderation is encouraged. Eating starch and vegetables only has a similar effect. So, it seems that if food combining works, it is because it is the opposite of what it calls itself: it is a food excluding diet. And when you exclude edible items such as bread, sugar, or alcohol, there will be a marked change of some sort on the amount of food you can consume, if only a placebo effect because you think it is helping. This is similar to the idea that you shouldn't drink a lot of water with your food because it interferes with digestion.

NEVER SKIP BREAKFAST:

Usually this is good advice as setting up the body for a day of activity by feeding it properly means one is less likely to eat stupidly when suddenly hungry—or when confronted with the hot doughnut stand at work. Skipping breakfast may be a good idea, however, if you've only got time for a sugary treat before you leave the house in the morning. It could be a better idea to grab a healthier, more lasting breakfast with less blood-sugar-messing sucrose than to stuff down a toaster waffle with maple syrup. It matters what kind of breakfast and what kind of schedule you have to really determine whether never skipping breakfast would actually help your weight loss in the long run. 🖫

GAS A PENNY A GALLON

In 1916, before the threat of global warming had become such an issue, the world's need to source a substitute for gasoline was not as pressing as it is today. Nevertheless, people have always been on the lookout for a bargain, so when American Louis Enricht announced that he had found a way to produce a cheap substitute for gasoline that could be manufactured for a penny a gallon, it aroused a great deal of interest.

Enricht's claim was that all he had to do to create gasoline was simply introduce a secret additive in the form of a green pill to ordinary tap water and create gasoline. That "secret" ingredient was his own invention, of course.

Offering to demonstrate his discovery in front of a group of reporters, he asked them to check over his demonstration car to verify that it had only one gas tank and that this was empty. He asked one of the reporters to bring him a bucket of ordinary tap water and then added his magic substance to it. He filled up the car's tank and started the engine. It ran smoothly and he took the reporters off for a short run.

As a result of this successful demonstration, a number of people offered to invest in Enricht's new discovery and money started to pour in. Even Henry Ford reportedly expressed an interest in buying the formula—along with Hiram Maxim of the Maxim Munitions Corporation. A wealthy railroad executive named Benjamin Yoakum reputedly contributed $100,000.

Unfortunately for Enricht, that deal went bad and the formula was found to be a fake. Enricht managed to avoid being taken to court on this occasion, but repeated the scam again in 1920, announcing that he had found a way to produce gasoline from peat. Once more the scheme attracted a great deal of attention, but an attorney delved into Enricht's background which proved to be dubious—he had been indicted for fraud in 1903—and found that, instead of spending the new investors' money on further research, Enricht had gone on a gambling spree. Water could not be turned into gasoline after all, not even with peat. This time Enricht was taken to court successfully and tried for grand larceny. Found guilty he was sentenced to 7 years imprisonment, but didn't serve his full term. Already elderly, he was paroled for reasons of ill health.

So how did he do it? It is possible that the magic ingredients added to the water were acetone and acetylene, which would enable the engine to be run for a short time but that would ultimately ruin it. Ironically, however, had Enricht's mixture been manufactured on a commercial scale, it would have been much more expensive than real gas. ✎

OBSCENE ROCK MYTHS EXPLODED

Judas Priest included subliminal satanic messages in their 1978 album
Stained Class

In a court case concerning such things, Priest guitarist K. K. Downing claimed "It'll be another 10 years before I can even spell subliminal."

The Rolling Stones beat up The Beatles backstage at *The Ed Sullivan Show*
in 1964

Not only were they never on the same bill for that show, but it's highly unlikely the Stones would have won in a fight.

NWA's *Efil4zaggin'* album is obscene

In 1991, the Obscene Publications squad raided Polygram's warehouse and impounded 12,500 copies of the LP, but in a court case some 4 months later magistrates threw out the charges, gave the albums back, and awarded costs to the record company. This is all in spite of the tracklisting containing such titles as "To Kill A Hooker" and "Findum Fuckum and Flee." 🖫

HORSE LIES #2

The spotted horses of the Nez Perce tribe were noted by Lewis and Clark as being the equal of any European horse, despite being some thousands of miles away from Europe in the plains of America's Rocky Mountains. Noted for their stamina and speed, the Appaloosa horse became popular in more modern times because of their distinctive coloration: they are the Dalmatians of the equine world. Like any other animal that achieves popularity in domesticity, the Appaloosa breed became known for its color and its kind disposition as well as its athletic ability. But, with its popularity came a decline of the breed's disposition. Because of bad breeding habits—people selecting the horses for their color rather than better horsie traits such as a happy disposition or a soundness of mind—Appaloosas became the Dalmatian/Irish Setter cross of the equine world: they were spotted *and* they were stupid, so much so that the old joke went, "Why did the Nez Perce chiefs ride their horses into battle?" Answer: "So they'd be good and angry by the time they got there." This is not unique to horse breeds. Every breed claims to be gentle, calm, and suitable for young riders. Very few breeds are. Even the Shetland, one of the oldest and smallest breeds of pony, can be exceedingly stubborn, smart, and bullying to people and to horses 4 times their size.

HOLLYWOOD IS A FAMILY TOWN

Edward Norton has to show his mother every script he is offered and then wait to see if she says he can accept the part or not. If he can, she goes through all his dialog.

Mel Gibson has 27 children and they're all named Christopher, even the girls.

Ben Affleck and Jennifer Lopez called off their wedding because of his constant refusal to eat anything other than blue food, and so he wouldn't be able to pose for the traditional pictures of the bride feeding cake to the groom.

William, Alec, and Stephen Baldwin are all the same person, and Adam Baldwin is the brother he "doesn't talk about." The typecast heavy is, in fact, no relation. 🖥♠

COINING IT

Two or 3 centuries ago, a Brit down on his luck and in need of a few extra shillings, guineas, or doubloons could always try his hand at "coining." The most common form of coining, or counterfeiting coins, was "clipping," which involved nicking very small pieces of gold or silver off the coin or filing it down slightly. The tiny pieces of precious metal were then collected and melted down to form new coins. In order to prevent this, in 1662 the British authorities introduced "milling," a process in which small grooves were cut into the coin rim at regular intervals. But this had little effect and the practice was still widespread. The coiners simply re-milled the slightly smaller (although not noticeably so) original coins. Coiner gangs operated up and down the country, producing both British and foreign coins (French, Spanish, or Portuguese), since all were legal tender in Britain at the time. A similar situation existed in the U.S. where Dutch Guilders and Spanish Dollars, Cobbs, and Reals were also in circulation. 🖎

FRANKLIN D. ROOSEVELT KNEW ABOUT THE ATTACK ON PEARL HARBOR

Conspiracists believe that American President Roosevelt knew that the Japanese were going to attack the American fleet at Pearl Harbor up to 3 days before they did in 1941. This is a lie. U.S. intelligence had picked up unspecific messages about an attack but had no idea of where or when it would happen. 📖

LIES COUPLES TELL #3

As with the Lies Women Tell Men, the course of human relationships and particularly those involving love, rarely run true. The following are examples of some of the lies that men and women tell each other when they're in love.

"SHE'S AN OLD FRIEND."

Old friends are the most suspicious because of their familiarity with your partner. Also, old friends have their own world which usually excludes partners, families, and such. Old friends know things about your partner you may never know, shameful, awful things. Given that, he or she has an inside track on your partner that you do not. Even worse, old friends are the kind of people to whom you cannot really object. Trying to stop your partner from seeing an old friend makes you look needy and jealous. Despite the fact that this may be so, you don't need to have that bit of information broadcast to your social circle. If she/he is an old friend, get them around for dinner. That's civilized.

"SHE'S GOING THROUGH TOUGH TIMES . . ."

Going through tough times usually means 2 things: your partner has a good excuse to see this old friend of theirs to offer support, and they will probably see each other more than once. A supportive friend is yet another thing you cannot begrudge your spouse without looking like a jerk. Of course, you trust him with her! Of course it is good that he is offering her his shoulder to cry on. And of course, you understand that your partner can't exactly leave a good friend in need. That said, how much support does this person actually require? If it involves underwear on hotel floors, maybe you and your partner need to talk about differences in the use of the word "help."

"I WAS GOING TO CALL BUT . . ."

You can fill in the rest of this lie yourself . . . "but I was having too much torrid sexual fun to think of you." Not taking the time to call can, of course, mean that they don't want to be at your beck and call. But mostly, not calling when they thought about calling means, in the words of a teen who stayed out late, didn't call on purpose, and worried his parents to death, "Let 'em sweat." Calls are nice to get, certainly, but they are also an annoying duty, especially to someone who may have more things on their mind than their relationship. Only you can tell whether this excuse is a lie or not. Either way, you didn't rate a call. You lost the power struggle.

"WHAT SECOND CELL PHONE?"

Discovering extra bills that you didn't know about? Be afraid, be very afraid. If
you scratch a little further into the pile of bills, you may see even more
suspicious costs. Hotels, flowers, candy, lingerie, department store bills, taxis,
hotels, dinners out (when he was supposed to be working), car rental, or even
plane fare. All of these things could add up to a mistress or lover who is getting
far better treatment than you warrant. Confronting your partner is one way to
handle it. If they answer, "I have no idea what those charges are . . ." then you
look like a fool. Calling the card company yourself, saying you are the card
holder's wife or secretary, can sometimes work. Calling the shop itself works
better. If you are at all suspicious, that is what you must be prepared to do.

"YOU'RE THE BOSS."

Actually, I *am,* but I am so sick and tired of being with a bully that I will allow
you to *think* you are the boss. Giving someone else the power to run the decision
machine can often create a new surge of energy in a relationship. The other
person suddenly gets their way and feels, in an ideal world, a sense of elation
and generosity of spirit. ❀

THE MARVELOUS BOY

In literary circles, Thomas Chatterton is regarded as the first of the great English Romantic poets, yet he was also an accomplished liar and fraud.

Born in 1752 in Bristol, Chatterton was a young man with a febrile imagination. Brought up by his widowed mother, he developed a passion for all things medieval, an interest he could pursue avidly in the city's old churches, poring over ancient manuscripts in the candle-lit gloom.

By the age of 11, he had become so steeped in medievalism that he was able to produce his first mock-medieval poem. This would have been a marvelous achievement at such a tender age by anyone's reckoning, but he chose to pass it off as a genuine, old manuscript. Chatterton subsequently penned a series of poems that he attributed to a 15th-century monk called Thomas Rowley, extolling the virtues of courtly love and lauding chivalrous deeds. Claiming that he had found the manuscripts in a box of old papers in a Bristol church, Chatterton somehow managed to convince a good number of his fellow citizens of their authenticity.

Chatterton left school and became apprenticed to an attorney. He decided to seek the patronage of fellow liar and author Horace Walpole and sent him some of the Rowley poems. (Walpole had written what would be regarded as the first gothic novel, *The Castle of Otranto* but, fearing rejection, he had claimed to have translated it from a 16th-century Italian original.) At first Walpole was impressed by the Rowley works but when his literary colleagues expressed outrage at the young man's audacity, Walpole wrote to reprimand Chatterton and advised him to seek a more honest career.

Disregarding this advice, in 1770 Chatterton made his way to London where he tried to establish himself as a professional writer. He managed to secure some work, including writing pieces for political journals, making good use of his caustic wit and talent for satire, but his income was low and the money slow coming in. Later that same year he was found dead in his lodgings from poison. He was just seventeen years of age.

Chatterton was the prototype tragic teen idol. Quite apart from the obvious tragedy of a talented young man dying so young, there is an ironic twist to this particular tale.

The Rowley poems, as they became known, were published to great acclaim in 1777 and many of the Romantic poets who came after him cited Chatterton's work as an important influence. Praised by Coleridge and Blake, Keats dedicated *Endymion* to him and Wordsworth famously called him "the marvellous boy." ✍

DIRTY TRICKS OF THE WINE TRADE #2

As with the winemaker who makes wine out of grapes that were supposed to be disposed of and renames it, "The Golden Harvest" or somesuch, many tricks come down to marketing. And the fact that the wine world is closed and looks after its own means that established producers who are suspected of bad practice are unlikely to be found out, because the messenger would get frozen out of the world which he or she relies on for a living. One well-known producer in California made a white wine that was not good. Their response was to remove it from the shelves, hang on to it for 5 years, rename it, and put it back on the shelves. It is still there. ⧗

PHONES ARE A GOOD THING, BECAUSE:

Everyone actually needs a cell phone.

Call centers make life easier.

Cell phones cause explosions at gasoline pumps.

"Texting" is the new poetry.

"Your call is valuable to us," especially since you're on hold for 45 minutes at a premium rate. ▣◆

THE CROWN JEWELS
IN THE TOWER OF LONDON ARE FAKE

The real ones were sold off to pay for Charles and Diana's wedding. 🖫🌑

ANIMAL LIES OR TRUTH #4

Lie: Sloths are lazy.
Truth: They move slowly because they have disproportionately weak muscles and a ver-r-r-y sl-o-o-ow metabolism.

Lie: Bats are blind.
Truth: Bats actually have very good eyesight, it's just that their hearing is better, therefore accurate navigation by echolocation is possible and they can fly quickly and safely in the dark.

Lie: Moths are drawn to flames.
Truth: Moths navigate by the moon, and when they see another light they think it is the moon.

Lie: Kangaroos box.
Truth: They might stand up and wave their forelegs about, or playfully wrestle with each other, but they use their powerful hindlegs to kick.

Lie: Beluga caviar comes from the eggs of the rare white beluga whale.
Truth: Whales are mammals, therefore they don't lay eggs.

Lie: Migrating birds travel in the flying vee formation because only one of them knows the way.
Truth: Actually it's to conserve energy as they are flying in the slip stream of the bird in front so as to avoid turbulence, and they will regularly change the lead. 🖫

JULIANNE MOORE IS A NATURAL REDHEAD

Revisit her full frontal scene in Robert Altman's 1983 film *Short Cuts* if you want indisputable celluloid proof. 🖫

LIES WE TELL OURSELVES #4

As much as we may tell untruths to the government, our parents, partners, or children, we may also tell ourselves lies. Because we have to and because it makes us feel better about ourselves.

✣ ✣ ✣

"I am not getting older, I am getting better."—No, you are just getting older. Even extremely young people worry about aging and what will happen in their lives. Telling yourself the wonderful lie that you are getting better with age is fooling yourself into thinking you are a fine wine. In this day of youth power, getting old is the worst thing you can do. The problem is that it is also inevitable. You weren't good when you were younger, so why not lie to yourself that you are getting better before you die? Because it is still a lie. The truth here is that you are, like the rest of us, only getting closer to your maker. Similar self-lie: "I am still young, I have all the time in the world."

✣ ✣ ✣

"She/He still loves me."—If you have to reassure yourself that someone loves you, they don't. Love does not need reassurance. Like trust, it is an intangible link between two or more people. Like animals, love is something we trust instinctively. By telling yourself that someone still loves you, you are lying to yourself that you still have someone to whom you can plead in times of trouble, or in times when you are unlovable even to your own mother. The lie of the ever-loving friend or partner allows us to feel we can do whatever damage we want to them and still expect them to accept us with their open arms. Love can be damaged. Lies like this stop us from seeing that.

✣ ✣ ✣

"I can handle this. I don't need any help."—There's nothing wrong with asking for help. Assistance can solve many problems easier, faster, and better than being proud and making mistakes on your own. This little self-told lie acts as a ghostly hand on the troubled one's shoulder, a kind of artificial self-steadying, which really does not help anything. The only action that it can engender is that of self-deception and denial. If you are having to make a mantra out of "handling something yourself" then it is fairly obvious that you can't. Meeting one's limitations and dealing with them is a sign of maturity and wisdom. Making good decisions has value. Pretending you're all right perpetuates the problem. ✤

FAT IS BAD

Although Robert Atkins died clinically obese at 258 lbs, what his books did not include was the conclusion that scientists are now reaching: that fat should be regarded as our friend. It helps the body to function properly.

Not only does fat protect the bones and organs, but it regulates the body's energy levels by producing the hormone leptin. Left to its own devices, this tells the brain whether we need to eat or stop eating. An absence of leptin can be particularly dangerous where pregnant women are concerned.

Simon Coppack from St. Bartholemew's Hospital and the Royal London School of Medicine goes so far as to say that fat should be regarded as an organ much like the liver, rather than as we often see it—as undesirable excess tissue. It even plays a role in the reproductive cycle: anorexic girls and women do not menstruate.

Leptin also helps to regulate our immune systems. It is so "smart," in fact, that it can temporarily suppress our appetite enabling our body to concentrate its energy on fighting infection. ⧗

SÉANCE TRICKS

The success of the popular 19th-century entertainment, the séance, relied upon the trickery of the medium and the credulity of the believer. Parlors were fitted with the types of equipment used by magicians. "Apports," gifts from the spirits, could be hidden around the room and accomplices of the medium would rap out messages. In the darkness of the séance, spirits could be conjured using cloth that had been coated with luminous paint. "Ectoplasm," a substance from the spirit world, would in fact be chiffon or gauze. Spirit photographs were easily produced using double exposures. The effect would be all the greater if actual likenesses of the deceased could be acquired beforehand and recreated in the séance. ✍

STEALTH ADVERTISING

Do you know when you are being manipulated by advertisers?

In recent years, some of the methods used by advertisers have become increasingly subtle, or, you could say, increasingly dishonest.

Advertisers will now actually hire bright young things to act as "plants" in an attempt to increase the attractiveness of their products. These hired hands pick up the product admiringly and enthusiastically in a store, for example, and so make onlookers similarly excited and curious about the product in question.

The other consumers have no idea what is going on but if they did would they object? You might think so but in fact research carried out into the subject suggests that we don't really care too much about being sold to in this way. Maybe we're just so accepting of the fact that we are being conned by advertisers and marketeers these days that the particular method of deception matters very little. ⏳

THE ZINOVIEV LETTER

The outcome of the 1924 British General Election was almost certainly influenced by a forged letter, purporting to come from Grigory Zinoviev, the head of the Communist International, Comintern. It was addressed to the Communist Party of Great Britain, urging it to intensify its subversive activities. The letter was leaked to the *Daily Mail* and published 4 days before the country voted. Headed "Very Secret," the letter was addressed to his British "Dear Comrades." If it was designed to create an anti-Communist scare, it succeeded. In the election, Britain's first Labour government, under Prime Minister Ramsay MacDonald, was defeated.

There were suspicions over the authenticity of the "Zinoviev letter" from the outset. Labour leaders denounced it as a forgery and the Soviet authorities agreed. Its true authorship wasn't established until the 1960s, when it was revealed that it had been perpetrated by a group of anti-Bolshevik Russian émigrés. ✑

INDEX

ACKNOWLEDGMENTS

Thanks to the following writers for contributing to this book:

Lloyd Bradley ....
Emma Hooley ....
Thomas Eaton ....
Karen Krizanovich ....
Jane Phillimore ....
Jackie Strachan ....